True OR FALSE?

Non-fiction for secondary English

PETER ELLISON

Hodder & Stoughton
A MEMBER OF THE HODDER HEADLINE GROUP

British Library Cataloguing in Publication Data
True or False?
  I. Ellison, Peter
  428.6

ISBN 0 340 62733 6

First published 1995
Impression number   10 9 8 7 6 5 4 3 2
Year   1999 1998 1997 1996

Copyright © 1995 Peter Ellison

All rights reserved. No part of this publication may be reproduced or transmitted in any form or by any means, electronic or mechanical, including photocopy, recording, or any information storage and retrieval system, without permission in writing from the publisher or under licence from the Copyright Licensing Agency Limited. Further details of such licences (for reprographic reproduction) may be obtained from the Copyright Licensing Agency Limited, of 90 Tottenham Court Road, London W1P 9HE.

Typeset by Wearset, Boldon, Tyne and Wear.
Printed in Great Britain for Hodder & Stoughton Educational, a division of Hodder Headline Plc, 338 Euston Road, London NW1 3BH by Bath Press Ltd, Bath.

Acknowledgements

The authors and publishers would like to thank the following for their kind permission to reproduce copyright material:

Marion Boyars Publishers Ltd for 'The Marabout's Saliva' from *Voices of Marrakech* by Elias Canetti; John Brown Publishing Ltd for 'Riddle of the Vanishing Woodsman', first published in the *Fortean Times*; Canongate Press Ltd for 'Betty the Hen' from *Spring Remembered* by Evelyn Cowan; Carcanet Press Ltd for 'Meeting Mr Ford' from *Tales of an Old Horse Trader* by Leroy Judson Daniels; Robert Chesshyre for 'Skelmersdale' from his book *Return of a Native Reporter*; Curtis Brown Ltd for 'Bombay' from *Flowers of Emptiness* by Sally Belfrage © Sally Belfrage; The Department of Transport for statistical material about child pedestrian casualties in 'From Home to School'; Andre Deutsch Ltd for 'Books and Father' from *The Tongue Set Free* by Elias Canetti; Faber and Faber Ltd for 'Beatings at the Dragon' from *Stand Before Your God* by Paul Watkins; *The Guardian* for the article 'Safety Fears Prompt Parents to Limit Children's Mobility, Research Shows' by Rebecca Smithers, 17 July, 1994; HarperCollins Publishers Ltd for 'A Kirghiz Dinner' by Ella Maillart from *A Book of Traveller's Tales*, editor Eric Newby; A M Heath and Co Ltd for 'Wounded' from *Homage to Catalonia* by George Orwell © The estate of the late Sonia Brownell Orwell and Martin Secker and Warburg; Herald Group of Newspapers for 'Craze for Video' first published in *Hoddesdon, Hertford and Ware Herald and Post*, 17 June, 1993; Ewan MacNaughton Associates for 'Parents Urged not to Smack Children' by Michael Kerr, *Daily Telegraph*, December 1990 © The Telegraph plc, London 1994; The Meat and Livestock Commission for 'Developments in Animal Welfare' and 'Variation in Nutrient Content of Popular Lunch-time Snacks' from *Meat in the News*; Newspaper Publishing plc for the following articles first published in *The Independent*: 'Don't Panic it's only Dr Robotnic' by Jane Berthoud, 'Dr Mario Made Me an Addict' by Bryan Appleyard, 16 June, 1993, 'Gamegirl Zapped' by Phil Dourado, 'Granny Falls for the Plumber' by Ian MacKinnon, and 'Hooked on Sonic the Hedgehog' by Jane Berthoud, 16 February, 1993; Oxford University Press for 'Lepelstraat' from *Bitter Herbs* by Marga Minco, translated from the Dutch by Roy Edwards (1960) © Oxford University Press 1960; Penguin Books Ltd for 'Books' from *Smile Please* by Jean Rhys; The Peters Fraser and Dunlop Group Ltd for 'First Moments in Prison' from *Dialogue With Death* by Arthur Koestler; Random House UK Ltd for 'Morning at Newton' from *Nairn in Darkness and in Light* by David Thomson; Reed Consumer Books Ltd for 'Las Vegas' from *The Lost Continent* by Bill Bryson, published by Secker & Warburg; Solo Syndication and Literary Agency Ltd for 'The Sega Sickener' by Luke Harding, first published in *Daily Mail*; The Vegetarian Society for *Space Sheep and Astro Pig*; Virago Press Ltd for 'The Belly-band of the World' from *Dust Tracks on a Dirt Road* by Zora Neale Hurston; The Women's Press Ltd for 'Thief!' from *To the Is-land* by Janet Frame. The author and publishers would also like to thank *The Sunday Times* for their permission to reproduce the *Joy Stick* cartoon 'I'm bored with video games' (p. 108) first published in *The Funday Times* © Times Newspapers/Supplements Limited, 1995.

Every effort has been made to trace and acknowledge ownership of copyright. The Publishers will be glad to make suitable arrangements with any copyright holders whom they have been unable to contact.

CONTENTS

Part 1 – Genre

My life

Morning at Newton	*David Thomson*	4
On vacation with father	*Bill Bryson*	8
Thief!	*Janet Frame*	13
First confession	*Tobias Wolff*	18
The belly-band of the world	*Zora Neale Hurston*	24

Books and me

Memories of early reading:		31
Books	*Jean Rhys*	31
Nicholas Nickleby	*Paul Bailey*	32
Books and Father	*Elias Canetti*	34
Harry the Hedgehog	*Karen Armstrong*	36

It was like this

Captured by Indians	*Hannah Swarton*	39
Two experiences of the Spanish Civil War:		41
First moments in prison	*Arthur Koestler*	41
Wounded	*George Orwell*	45
Lepelstraat	*Marga Minco*	49

Contents

Travellers' tales

Vale Perilous	*Sir John Mandeville*	54
The marabout's saliva	*Elias Canetti*	59
A Kirghiz dinner	*Ella Maillart*	63
First impressions:		66
Bombay	*Sally Belfrage*	66
Las Vegas	*Bill Bryson*	68
Skelmersdale	*Robert Chesshyre*	72

Part 2 – Issues

Animals

Betty the Hen	*Evelyn Cowan*	80
Space Sheep and Astro Pig	*The Vegetarian Society*	84
The other side:		
Developments in Animal Welfare		
The Meat and Livestock Commission		88

The effects of Mr Ford

Meeting Mr Ford	*Leroy Judson Daniels*	94
From home to school	*The Guardian*	98

Computer games

What adults think	*The Independent, Daily Mail, The Herald*	103
What *is* the problem?	*The Independent, The Herald*	109
Game language		112
Game names		113

It never did me any harm

No smacking week	*Daily Mirror, Daily Telegraph*	117
Beatings at the Dragon	*Paul Watkins*	122

Part 1
GENRE

My Life

You are often asked to write about your own experiences or memories at school, so you will know that autobiographical writing (writing about yourself) is not easy. How do you make your writing both truthful and entertaining?

All the writers in this unit have faced this very problem. Some of them see their lives as comical, others try to recreate the deep-felt emotions of a distant childhood. The suggestions for writing that follow the extracts may be put together at the end of the unit to produce a mini autobiography of your own.

Part One – Genre

Morning at Newton

In the following extract, David Thomson writes about growing up in a large house (Newton) in Nairn, a small fishing town in the Highlands of Scotland.

Our summer mornings at Newton have melted into one idyllic morning. I awoke at about six on my narrow bed in my father's dressing room which opened through a door into the wide bedroom where he and my mother slept in a four-poster bed. Probably it was a two-poster, with curtains at the pillow end and none at the foot. The bedroom and dressing room faced north-east and the early sun slanted across our windows. As I lay in bed all I saw was the sea and the dark cliffs of the Black Isle far away broken in the middle by the entrance to Cromarty Firth. As I sat up I saw the yellow oat field and the rich smooth golf links which sloped steeply down to the beach. When I jumped out of bed and ran to the window I saw the great green lawn, sheltered by pine woods on either side, sloping away to the edge of the oatfield from which it was divided by a wire fence on wooden posts. Below me was the semi-circle of dark grey stone steps which went down between balustrades from the huge front door to the gravelled circle into which Newton's front and back drives led.

   At about seven o'clock I would creep out of the room to meet my sisters on the landing, tiptoeing in my bare feet past my parents' bed, hoping not to wake them; but Mother was often awake by then and pushing the bed curtain back with her bare arm, would pull me to her and kiss me. 'You'll never find your fruit today,' she sometimes whispered. 'You'll have to look in places where you've never looked before!' Knowing that breakfast was not till nine o'clock she made provision for our early mornings just before she went to bed each night, by placing biscuits, apples, black or red currants from the garden, plums from the wall or peaches and grapes from the two vast greenhouses which stood against the southern boundary of the vegetable garden; and these four little heaps of bright delicacy, one for each of us and each composed of different fruits, she hid in a new place every night. Our search behind the curtains of the staircase windows, behind the bowls and ornaments on the hall table, in the carved woodwork of the grandfather clock by the front door, on top of the brass fire extinguishers which hung from the walls of the wide and long passages on the ground floor, was exciting and difficult. Each of us took possession of the first heap found and began at once to eat while the others went on searching. My sisters, who had good eyesight, gave me hints in riddle language if they saw me in despair, and often we would share or swap our treasures. Mary or Joan, the two elder ones, would lift up our little sister Barbara to enable her to find her portion in high places. There were small doors in the wooden panelling giving access to pipes and bellwires. Barbara thought they had been made to help the mice to come out for crumbs and get back in safety to their dark nests.

Running through the long corridor that leads from the front door to the back of the house, we would turn to the right into a narrower and darker one, laid with the same thick Indian carpet, red with gold and black patterns on it, until we came to the double doorway that led to a stone stairway, similarly curved but smaller than the one at the front of the house. Running swiftly across the gravel path on to the back lawn, we came to a lily pond and fountain in the middle made of white stone. I cannot remember the fountain playing. It had

probably broken down from neglect during the four years of the war, those first four years of my life. Our bare feet left a lovely tread on the dew, as on ice but transparent, and looking back on them we could see how we had separated clusters of dewdrops, some silvery, some crystal clear, some with the colours of the rainbow shining in them. We went deep into the woods and gathered fir cones, birds' feathers and sticks when we found strangely shaped ones. We climbed trees, then went into the orchard and ate apples which were sour and unripe in August, with white pips.

As soon as we guessed it was near feeding time we walked back towards the

Part One – Genre

house and round it, through the stable yard and under an archway between low buildings to the hen yard to watch the henwife feed the geese, ducks and hens. She lived in one of those low buildings overlooking this yard and emerged from the darkness of her doorway like a fat mole, hunched, covered from head to thigh by a heavy grey shawl with a long black dress beneath it, under which as she hobbled along you could see bits of her black boots stained with poultry muck and ashes from her fire. When she was in a good mood she would allow us to scatter some of the grain or fill troughs with mash, but we feared and hated her, partly because of her hostility towards us, and the vicious bad temper with which she treated any servant from the house who was sent to give her instructions, but mostly because she was ostentatiously cruel. We often watched her killing poultry, my sisters by chance when they happened to be passing the hen yard at those times, I, occasionally and in secret, by design; for the sight and sounds aroused an emotional tension in me which was at once repellent and attractive. I would think about it in bed with sorrow and compassion for the bird and yet I would long for the day when I would be old enough to kill one with my own hands. The henwife would catch a bird roughly, handle it harshly before it was dead, then kill it slowly by wringing its neck in the old-fashioned way, instead of dislocating the neck with one pull which causes instant death. I believe she relished the agonies of her victims.

The little we could see of her face beneath the shawl was cruel: tiny black eyes that gleamed and were rounded like hatpin heads, lips as thin as razors and blue, a revolting button of a nose which looked as though someone had cut its tip off with a pair of curved scissors. Her moustache was thick and short, her beard wispy: both grey. She killed prime chickens, capons, old hens for boiling, ducks, geese, guinea-fowl, as the cook, Mrs Waddell, ordered them. Mrs Waddell needed much meat, fish and fowl to feed us, our many uncles and aunts, the numerous household servants and all those guests whom Uncle Robert invited to spend the summer vacation at Newton.

David Thomson, *Nairn in Darkness and Light*

My life

Talking points

- The first three paragraphs of this extract make Newton seem like heaven. What is it in the writing that gives this impression?

    Take a piece of paper and mark out five columns, one for each of the five senses – sight, hearing, touch, taste, smell. In each column, note down any words or phrases from the extract that appeal to that sense.

    Which columns fill up quickly? Does any column remain empty?

- The fourth and fifth paragraphs are very different from the first three. Why does the author find the henwife so disgusting?

    Many children become frightened of old people in their neighbourhood – often harmless old women or men – just because of the way they look. Do you have any memories of people like that?

Suggestions for writing

1 Write about a particular summer morning that you remember. It could be during a summer holiday when you woke up in a strange bed and looked out of your bedroom window for the first time, or it could be an ordinary summer's day at home.

    Like the author of the extract, use the senses to conjure up the atmosphere of that perfect summer morning.

2 Write about a character in your neighbourhood whom children find both fascinating and frightening. Describe an episode when you came into contact with him or her.

3 Write a piece that combines beauty and happiness with ugliness and fear, as the extract does. Concentrate on creating an atmosphere of beauty and perfection in the first part of your writing. Then change it.

Your description could be autobiographical or fictional. Here are two ideas to help you:

- A walk on a beautiful sunny day is spoiled by the sight of a dead animal.
- A child playing in the garden hears his or her parents arguing.

Part One – Genre

On vacation with Father

Summer holidays are important times for children and often remain in the memory for a long time. They can be absolutely wonderful, but they can also be times when parents inflict the most terrible suffering on their captive offspring!

This was the case for Bill Bryson, whose father made summer holidays a testing time for his wife and children.

My father liked Iowa. He lived his whole life in the state, and is even now working his way through eternity there, in Glendale Cemetery in Des Moines. But every year he became seized with a quietly maniacal urge to get out of the state and go on vacation. Every summer, without a whole lot of notice, he would load the car to groaning, hurry us into it, take off for some distant point, return to get his wallet after having driven almost to the next state, and take off again for some distant point. Every year it was the same. Every year it was awful.

The big killer was the tedium. Iowa is in the middle of the biggest plain this side of Jupiter. Climb onto a roof-top almost anywhere in the state and you are confronted with a featureless sweep of corn for as far as the eye can see. It is 1,000 miles from the sea in any direction, 400 miles from the nearest mountain, 300 miles from skyscrapers and muggers and things of interest, 200 miles from people who do not habitually stick a finger in their ear and swivel it around as a preliminary to answering any question addressed to them by a stranger. To reach anywhere of even passing interest from Des Moines by car requires a journey that in other countries would be considered epic. It means days and days of unrelenting tedium, in a baking steel capsule on a ribbon of highway.

In my memory, our vacations were always taken in a big *blue* Rambler station-wagon. It was a cruddy car – my dad always bought cruddy cars, until he got to the male menopause and started buying zippy red convertibles – but it had the great virtue of space. My brother, sister and I in the back were miles away from my parents up front, in effect in another room. We quickly discovered during illicit forays into the picnic hamper that if you stuck a bunch of Ohio Blue Tip matches into an apple or hard-boiled egg, so that it resembled a porcupine, and casually dropped it out the tailgate window, it was like a bomb. It would explode with a small bang and a surprisingly big flash of blue flame, causing cars following behind to veer in an amusing fashion.

My dad, miles away up front, never knew what was going on and could not understand why all day long cars would zoom up alongside him with the driver gesticulating furiously, before tearing off into the distance. 'What was that all about?' he would say to my mother in a wounded tone.

My life

'I don't know, dear,' my mother would answer mildly. My mother only ever said two things. She said, 'I don't know, dear.' And she said, 'Can I get you a sandwich, honey?' Occasionally on our trips she would volunteer other pieces of intelligence like, 'Should that dashboard light be glowing like that, dear?' or, 'I think you hit that dog/man/blind person back there, honey,' but mostly she wisely kept quiet. This was because on vacations my father was a man obsessed. His principal obsession was with trying to economise. He always took us to the crummiest hotels and motor lodges, and to the kind of roadside eating-houses where they only washed the dishes weekly. You always knew, with a sense of doom, that at some point before finishing you were going to discover someone else's congealed egg-yolk lurking somewhere on your plate or plugged between the tines of your fork. This, of course, meant cooties and a long, painful death.

But even that was a relative treat. Usually we were forced to picnic by the side of the road. My father had an instinct for picking bad picnic sites – on the apron of a busy truck stop or in a little park that turned out to be in the heart of some seriously deprived ghetto, so that groups of children would come and stand silently by our table and watch us eating Hostess Cupcakes and crinkle-cut potato chips – and it always became incredibly windy the moment we stopped, that my mother spent the whole of lunch-time chasing paper plates over an area of about an acre.

9

Part One – Genre

In 1957 my father invested $19.98 in a portable gas stove that took an hour to assemble before each use and was so wildly temperamental that we children were always ordered to stand well back when it was being lit. This always proved unnecessary, however, because the stove would flicker to life only for a few seconds before puttering out, and my father would spend many hours turning it this way and that to keep it out of the wind, simultaneously addressing it in a low, agitated tone normally associated with the chronically insane. All the while my brother, sister and I would implore him to take us some place with air-conditioning, linen table-cloths and ice-cubes clinking in glasses of clear water. 'Dad,' we would beg, 'you're a successful man. You make a good living. Take us to a Howard Johnson's.' But he wouldn't have it. He was a child of the Depression and where capital outlays were involved he always wore the haunted look of a fugitive who had just heard bloodhounds in the distance.

Eventually, with the sun low in the sky, he would hand us hamburgers that were cold and raw and smelled of butane. We would take one bite and refuse to eat any more. So my father would lose his temper and throw everything into the car and drive us at high speed to some roadside diner where a sweaty man with a floppy hat would sling hash while grease-fires danced on his grill. And afterwards, in a silent car filled with bitterness and unquenched basic needs, we would mistakenly turn off the main highway and get lost and end up in some no-hope hamlet with a name like Draino, Indiana, or Tapwater, Missouri, and get a room in the only hotel in town, the sort of rundown place where if you wanted to watch TV it meant you had to sit in the lobby and share a cracked leatherette sofa with an old man with big sweat circles under his arms. The old man would almost certainly have only one leg and probably one other truly arresting deficiency, like no nose or a caved-in forehead, which meant that although you were sincerely intent on watching *Laramie* or *Our Miss Brooks*, you found your gaze being drawn, ineluctably and sneakily, to the amazing eaten-away body sitting beside you. You couldn't help yourself. Occasionally the man would try to engage you in lively conversation. It was all most unsatisfying.

After a week or so of this kind of searing torment, we would fetch up at some blue and glinting sweep of lake or sea in a bowl of pine-clad mountains, a place full of swings and amusements and the gay shrieks of children splashing in water, and it would all almost be worth it. Dad would become funny and warm and even once or twice might take us out to the sort of restaurant where you didn't have to watch your food being cooked and where the glass of water they served you wasn't autographed with lipstick. This was living. This was heady opulence.

Bill Bryson, *The Lost Continent*

Talking points

- What impression do you get of the author's father from this extract?
  Here are some words to help you in your discussion. Choose the ones that you think describe him best:

obsessive	selfish	cruel	generous	mean
proud	obstinate	sensitive	frightening	kind
loving	pathetic		hot-tempered	

  Back your ideas up with evidence from the extract.

- What impression do you get of the author's mother from this extract?

- In your group, put together the impression of America that you get from this extract. How does it compare with the picture of America that you have built up from films and television, or maybe from your own holidays in America?

- Have you ever had any funny or disastrous holidays? Discuss your holiday experiences as a group and then choose one or two of the best experiences to tell to the rest of the class.

Suggestions for writing

1 Write about a disastrous holiday that you have been on. It may have been an unpleasant experience at the time, but with hindsight such holidays often become funny.

   Here are some common experiences to get you started:

   - the long airport wait
   - the terrible (unbuilt?) hotel
   - the arguments in the back of the car
   - the appalling food
   - the irritating people who follow you round the hotel trying to make friends
   - getting lost on the way there in the car
   - mistakes in a foreign language
   - dreadful weather.

Part One – Genre

2 The author of this extract uses this account of a typical holiday to write a portrait of his father. Choose a member of your family and use a similar technique to write about him or her. You do not have to write about holidays.

Here are some possible titles:

- Shopping with my brother
- Christmas with grandfather
- A bike ride with my sister
- A visit to the dentist with my little brother
- Gardening with my mother
- Fishing with my father.

Thief!

When you were a child, did you ever do something that made you ashamed? When you look back on it, the act often seems unimportant, but at the time it felt like the end of the world.

In the following extract Janet Frame, a writer from New Zealand, describes an event like this, when she was branded as a thief.

One morning, during my first week at school, I sneaked into Mum and Dad's bedroom, opened the top drawer of the duchesse, where the coins 'brought back from the war' were kept, and helped myself to a handful. I then went to Dad's best trousers hanging behind the door, put my hand in the pocket (how cold and slippery the lining!), and took out two coins. Hearing someone coming, I hastily thrust the money under the duchesse and left the room, and later, when the coast was clear, I retrieved my hoard and on my way to school stopped at Heath's store to buy some chewing gum.

Mr Heath looked sternly at me. 'This money won't buy anything,' he said. 'It's Egyptian.'

'I know,' I lied. Then, handing him the money from Dad's pocket, I asked, 'Will this buy me some chewing gum?'

'That's better,' he said, returning yet another of the coins, a farthing.

Armed with a supply of chewing gum, I waited at the door of the Infant Room, a large room with a platform or stage at one end and double doors opening on to Standard One, and as the children went into the room, I gave each a 'pillow' of chewing gum. Later, Miss Botting, a woman in a blue costume the same color as the castor-oil bottle, suddenly stopped her teaching and asked, 'Billy Delamare, what are you eating?'

'Chewing gum, Miss Botting.'

'Where did you get it?'

'From Jean Frame, Miss Botting.' (I was known at school as Jean and at home as Nini.)

'Dids McIvor, where did you get your chewing gum?'

'From Jean Frame, Miss.'

'Jean Frame, where did you get the chewing gum?'

'From Heath's, Miss Botting.'

'Where did you get the money?'

'My father gave it to me.'

Evidently Miss Botting did not believe me. Suddenly she was determined to get 'the truth' out of me. She repeated her question. 'Where did you get the money? I want the *truth*.'

I repeated my answer, substituting *Dad* for *father*.

Part One—Genre

'Come out here.'

I came out in front of the class.

'Go up on the platform.'

I went up on to the platform.

'Now tell me where you got the money.'

Determinedly I repeated my answer.

Playtime came. The rest of the class went out to play while Miss Botting and I grimly faced each other.

'Tell me the truth,' she said.

I replied, 'Dad gave me the money.'

She sent for Myrtle and Bruddie, who informed her with piping innocence that Dad did not give me the money.

'Yes, he did,' I insisted. 'He called me back when you had both gone to school.'

'He didn't.'

'He did.'

All morning I stayed on the platform. The class continued their reading lessons. I stayed on the platform through lunchtime and into the afternoon, still refusing to confess. I was beginning to feel afraid, instead of defiant, as if I hadn't a friend in the world, and because I knew that Myrtle and Bruddie would 'tell' as soon as they got home, I felt that I never wanted to go home. All the places I had found – the birch log in Glenham, the top of the climbers in Edendale, the places in the songs and poems – seemed to have vanished, leaving me with no place. I held out obstinately until mid-afternoon, when the light was growing thin with masses of dark tiredness showing behind it, and the schoolroom was filled with a nowhere dust, and a small voice answered from the scared me in answer to Miss Botting's repeated question: 'I took the money out of my father's pocket.'

While I'd been lying, I had somehow protected myself; I knew now that I had no protection. I'd been found out as a thief. I was so appalled by my future prospects that I don't remember if Miss Botting strapped me. I know she gave the news to the class, and it spread quickly around the school that I was a thief. Loitering at the school gate, wondering where to go and what to do, I saw Myrtle and Bruddie, carefree as ever, on their way home. I walked slowly along the cocksfoot-bordered road. I don't know when I had learned to read, but I had read and knew the stories in the primer books, and I thought of the story of the fox that sprang out from the side of the road and swallowed the child. No one knew what had happened or where the child had gone, until one day when the fox was walking by, a kind person heard, 'Let me out, let me out!' coming from the fox's belly, whereupon the kind person killed the fox, slit the belly open, and lo, the child emerged whole, unharmed, and was taken by the kind person to live in a wood in a cottage made of coconut ice with a licorice chimney . . .

I finally arrived at our place. Myrtle was leaning over the gate. 'Dad knows,' she said, in a matter-of-fact voice. I went up the path. The front door was open and Dad was waiting with the strap in his hand. 'Come into the bedroom,' he said sternly. He administered his usual 'hiding,' not excessive, as some children had, but sharp and full of anger that one of his children was a *thief. Thief, thief.* At home and at school I was now called *Thief.*

Another event that followed swiftly upon my stealing of fourpence and a handful of Egyptian coins and a farthing stays in my mind because even then I knew it to be a rich comment on the ways of the world. I was learning fast.

Margaret Cushen, the headmaster's daughter, with all the prestige attached to such a position, had a birthday. Miss Botting (still wearing the color of the castor-oil bottle and linked in my mind with the bluebottle blowflies), announcing Margaret's birthday, asked her to stand on the platform while we sang 'Happy Birthday to You.'

Then Miss Botting gave Margaret an envelope. 'It's a present from your father. Open it, Margaret.'

Margaret, flushed and proud, opened the envelope and withdrew a piece of paper that she held up for all to see. 'It's a pound note,' she said with astonished joy.

The class echoed, 'A pound note.'

'Now isn't Margaret a lucky girl to get a pound note from her father for her birthday?' Miss Botting appeared to be as excited and pleased as Margaret who, still waving her pound note, returned to her seat, stared at with awe, envy, and admiration by the rest of the class.

This sudden introduction to variations of treasure was more than I could comprehend; it is doubtful whether I had any clear thoughts about it; I had only confused feelings, wondering how money brought home from the war and clearly treasured could buy nothing, how a threepence and a penny were looked on by everyone as a fortune, and I as the thief of the fortune; yet people, especially fathers, gave their daughters pound notes for their birthdays, as if pound notes were both more and less valuable than fourpence. I wondered, too, about Miss Botting and why she had needed to keep me nearly all day on the stage, waiting for me to confess.

Janet Frame, *To the Is-land*

Part One – Genre

Talking points

- Why do you think the author stole the money?

- Do you think that Miss Botting's punishment of the author was fair? How would you have punished her?

- If you had been the author's parents, how would you have dealt with her crime?

- Why do you think the episode of the headmaster's daughter's birthday present has such a profound effect on the writer?

Suggestions for writing

1 Write about an experience when you got into trouble and were punished unfairly. You may have been guilty but felt that the punishment was too harsh; or you may have been innocent.

2 Write a story, set in school, in which someone is forced to face up to the fact that others are better off than he or she is. Here are some ideas to help you:

   - A new craze has hit the school, and everyone has bought it . . . with the exception of one member of the class.
   - A teacher asks the class to write about what they did on their holidays. Everyone is writing about a seaside or foreign holiday . . . except for one pupil.

   You could write the story from the point of view of the person who is left out.

3 Parts of Janet Frame's autobiography (from which this extract is taken) have been made into a film called *An Angel at my Table*.

   Here is one way of imaging the extract as a film without the aid of a camera.

   - Imagine that you had to use six still photographs to represent the 'Thief' episode (ending at 'I was now called *Thief*.'). With a partner, describe each 'photograph' in detail. The more detailed and effective you make your description, the more your readers will be able to 'see' the picture as they read.

For example, you could start like this:

Photo One:

Janet (Jean) is standing by a chest of drawers in her parents' bedroom. The drawer is slightly open, and she is staring at some coins in her hand. The light from the window is falling on the coins, and they are shining in her hand. There is a look of excitement on her face.

Or like this:

Janet is standing behind the door of her parents' bedroom. Her father's trousers are hanging up on the door. Janet's hand is in the trouser pocket. She has a look of concentration on her face as she searches in the pocket for coins.

Remember you can only use six photos, so choose carefully.

- Now do the same for the 'pound note' episode, but use only four 'photographs'.
- You could put extracts of dialogue next to your descriptions of 'photographs'. You could also describe the sounds that would go with the pictures, either as background sound effects or music.

When you have finished, compare your choice of 'photographs' with others'. Are there any similarities? Does your choice of 'photograph' make a difference to the meaning of the extract?

Part One—Genre

First confession

In Tobias Wolff's autobiography *This Boy's Life* he describes how he and his mother converted to Roman Catholicism. Sister James was appointed to give them instruction in the religion. After a while, she decided that the time had come for Tobias to take part in the most important event in a young Catholic's life: the first confession.

> **Before you read the extract, think about what it must be like for the first time, to go into a dark cubicle, with a priest on the other side of the partition, and confess your sins.**
>
> **If it was *your* first confession, what would *you* confess?**

I was baptized during Easter along with several others from my catechism class. To prepare ourselves for communion we were supposed to make a confession, and Sister James appointed a time that week for each of us to come to the rectory and be escorted by her to the confessional. She would wait outside until we were finished and then guide us through our penance.

I thought about what to confess, but I could not break my sense of being at fault down to its components. Trying to get a particular sin out of it was like fishing a swamp, where you feel the tug of something that at first seems promising and then resistant and finally hopeless as you realize that you've snagged the bottom, that you have the whole planet on the other end of your line. Nothing came to mind. I didn't see how I could go through with it, but in the end I hauled myself down to the church and kept my appointment. To have skipped it would have called attention to all my other absences and possibly provoked a visit from Sister James to my mother. I couldn't risk having the two of them compare notes.

Sister James met me as I was coming into the rectory. She asked if I was ready and I said I guessed so.

'It won't hurt,' she said. 'No more than a shot, anyway.'

We walked over to the church and down the side aisle to the confessional. Sister James opened the door for me. 'In you go,' she said. 'Make a good one now.'

I knelt with my face to the screen as we had been told to do and said, 'Bless me Father for I have sinned.'

I could hear someone breathing loudly on the other side. After a time he said, 'Well?'

I folded my hands together and closed my eyes and waited for something to present itself.

'You seem to be having some trouble.' His voice was deep and scratchy.

'Yes sir.'

'Call me Father. I'm a priest, not a gentleman. Now then, you understand that whatever gets said in here stays in here.'

'Yes, Father.'

'I suppose you've thought a lot about this. Is that right?'

I said that I had.

'Well, you've just given yourself a case of nerves, that's all. How about if we try again a little later. Shall we do that?'

'Yes please, Father.'

'That's what we'll do, then. Just wait outside a second.'

I stood and left the confessional. Sister James came toward me from where she'd been standing against the wall. 'That wasn't so bad now, was it?' she asked.

'I'm supposed to wait,' I told her.

She looked at me. I could see she was curious, but she didn't ask any questions.

The priest came out soon after. He was old and very tall and walked with a limp. He stood close beside me, and when I looked up at him I saw the white hair in his nostrils. He smelled strongly of tobacco. 'We had a little trouble getting started,' he said.

'Yes, Father?'

'He's just a bit nervous is all,' the priest said. 'Needs to relax. Nothing like a glass of milk for that.'

She nodded.

'Why don't we try again a little later. Say twenty minutes?'

'We'll be here, Father.'

Sister James and I went to the rectory kitchen. I sat at a steel cutting table while she poured me a glass of milk. 'You want some cookies?' she asked.

'That's all right, Sister.'

'Sure you do.' She put a package of Oreos on a plate and brought it to me. Then she sat down. With her arms crossed, hands hidden in her sleeves, she watched me eat and drink. Finally she said, 'What happened, then? Cat get your tongue?'

'Yes, Sister.'

'There's nothing to be afraid of.'

'I know.'

'Maybe you're just thinking of it wrong,' she said.

I stared at my hands on the tabletop.

'I forgot to give you a napkin,' she said. 'Go on and lick them. Don't be shy.'

She waited until I looked up, and when I did I saw that she was younger than I thought her to be. Not that I'd given much thought to her age. Except for the really old nuns with canes or facial hair they all seemed outside of time, without past or future. But now – forced to look at Sister James across the narrow space

Part One—Genre

of this gleaming table – I saw her differently. I saw an anxious woman of about my mother's age who wanted to help me without knowing what kind of help I needed. Her good will worked strongly on me. My eyes burned and my throat swelled up. I would have surrendered to her if only I'd known how.

'It probably isn't as bad as you think it is,' Sister James said. 'Whatever it is, someday you'll look back and you'll see that it was natural. But you've got to bring it to the light. Keeping it in the dark is what makes it feel so bad.' She added, 'I'm not asking you to tell me, understand. That's not my place. I'm just saying that we all go through these things.'

Sister James leaned forward over the table. 'When I was your age,' she said, 'maybe even a little older, I used to go through my father's wallet while he was taking his bath at night. I didn't take bills, just pennies and nickels, maybe a dime. Nothing he'd miss. My father would've given me the money if I'd asked for it. But I preferred to steal it. Stealing from him made me feel awful, but I did it all the same.'

She looked down at the tabletop. 'I was a backbiter, too. Whenever I was with one friend I would say terrible things about my other friends, and then turn around and do the same thing to the one I had just been with. I knew what I was doing, too. I hated myself for it, I really did, but that didn't stop me. I used to wish that my mother and my brothers would die in a car crash so I could grow up with just my father and have everyone feel sorry for me.'

Sister James shook her head. 'I had all these bad thoughts I didn't want to let go of. Know what I mean?'

I nodded, and presented her with an expression that was meant to register dawning comprehension.

'Good!' she said. She slapped her palms down on the table. 'Ready to try again?'

I said that I was.

Sister James led me back to the confessional. I knelt and began again: 'Bless me Father, for —'

'All right,' he said. 'We've been here before. Just talk plain.'

'Yes, Father.'

Again I closed my eyes over my folded hands.

'Come come,' he said, with a certain sharpness.

'Yes, Father.' I bent close to the screen and whispered, 'Father, I steal.'

He was silent for a moment. Then he said, 'What do you steal?'

'I steal money, Father. From my mother's purse when she's in the shower.'

'How long have you been doing this?'

I didn't answer.

'Well?' he said. 'A week? A year? Two years?'

I chose the one in the middle. 'A year.'

'A year,' he repeated. 'That won't do. You have to stop. Do you intend to stop?'

'Yes, Father.'

'Honestly, now.'

'Honestly, Father.'

'All right. Good. What else?'

'I'm a backbiter.'

'A backbiter?'

'I say things about my friends when they're not around.'

'That won't do either,' he said.

'No, Father.'

'That certainly won't do. Your friends will desert you if you persist in this and let me tell you, a life without friends is no life at all.'

'Yes, Father.'

'Do you sincerely intend to stop?'

'Yes, Father.'

Part One – Genre

'Good. Be sure that you do. I tell you this in all seriousness. Anything else?'
'I have bad thoughts, Father.'
'Yes. Well,' he said, 'why don't we save those for next time. You have enough to work on.'
The priest gave me my penance and absolved me. As I left the confessional I heard his own door open and close. Sister James came forward to meet me again, and we waited together as the priest made his way to where we stood. Breathing hoarsely, he steadied himself against a pillar. He laid his other hand on my shoulder. 'That was fine,' he said. 'Just fine.' He gave my shoulder a squeeze. 'You have a fine boy here, Sister James.'
She smiled. 'So I do, Father. So I do.'

Tobias Wolff, *This Boy's Life*

Talking points

- What do you think is the purpose of confession?

- At what point do you think that Tobias decides to lie to the priest?

- Do you feel that Tobias takes his religion seriously?

Here are some statements to help your discussion. Decide which you agree with and which you don't.

– Tobias does not believe in God.
– He has tricked Sister James and the priest.
– He will be punished for what he has done.
– He sincerely wants to confess.
– He wants to please Sister James.
– He is a liar.
– Tobias discovers that it is easier to lie than to be honest.
– He finds out that confessing sins is impossible.
– Tobias has committed a sin.
– Tobias believes he has never committed a sin.

Now, in groups, decide which *two* of these statements are the most important. When you have made your choice, compare your decision with those of other groups.

- Do you think that Sister James and the priest handled the author well? Could either of them have done or said anything that would have made him confess genuinely?

22

My life

Suggestions for writing

1 Many religions have rituals which show that a child has become an adult – Jews have the Barmitzvah, Christians have confirmation, and Catholics have first confession, as in the extract.

   Have you taken part in any religious ceremonies like these? If so, write about your experiences. How did it feel to go through such an important episode in your life?

2 If you have not taken part in religious ceremonies like these, write about any other important 'first times' in your life. For example, you could write about the first time you went away without your parents or your first 'date' with a boyfriend or girlfriend.

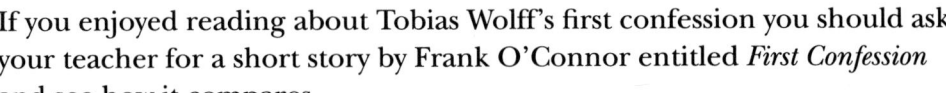

If you enjoyed reading about Tobias Wolff's first confession you should ask your teacher for a short story by Frank O'Connor entitled *First Confession* and see how it compares.

Part One – Genre

The belly-band of the world

All children have dreams of escaping from their humdrum daily lives. In her autobiography, *Dust Tracks on a Road*, Zora Neale Hurston explains that she had a strong imagination from an early age and often seemed to live in a fantasy world. In this extract from her book, her fantasies come into collision with the real world.

> Before you read about Hurston's childhood fantasies, take a moment to think about your own. Was there ever something that you *really* wanted but knew that you could never have?

For a long time I gloated over the happy secret that when I played outdoors in the moonlight the moon followed me, whichever way I ran. The moon was so happy when I came out to play, that it ran shining and shouting after me like a pretty puppy dog. The other children didn't count.

But I was rudely shaken out of this when I confided my happy secret to Carrie Roberts, my chum. It was cruel. She not only scorned my claim, she said that the moon was paying me no mind at all. The moon, my own happy private-playing moon, was out in its play yard to race and play with her.

We disputed the matter with hot jealousy, and nothing would do but we must run a race to prove which one the moon was loving. First, we both ran a race side by side, but that proved nothing because we both contended that the moon was going that way on account of us. I just knew that the moon was there to be with me, but Carrie kept on saying that it was herself that the moon preferred. So then it came to me that we ought to run in opposite directions so that Carrie could come to her senses and realize the moon was mine. So we both stood with our backs to our gate, counted three and tore out in opposite directions.

'Look! Look, Carrie!' I cried exultantly. 'You see the moon is following me!'

'Aw, youse a tale-teller! You know it's chasing me.'

So Carrie and I parted company, mad as we could be with each other. When the other children found out what the quarrel was about, they laughed it off. They told me the moon always followed them. The unfaithfulness of the moon hurt me deeply. My moon followed Carrie Roberts. My moon followed Matilda Clarke and Julia Moseley, and Oscar and Teedy Miller. But after a while, I ceased to ache over the moon's many loves. I found comfort in the fact that though I was not the moon's exclusive friend, I was still among those who showed the moon which way to go. That was my earliest conscious hint that the world didn't tilt under my footfalls, nor careen over one-sided just to make me glad.

But no matter whether my probings made me happier or sadder, I kept on probing to know. For instance, I had a stifled longing. I used to climb to the top

My life

of one of the huge chinaberry trees which guarded our front gate, and look out over the world. The most interesting thing that I saw was the horizon. Every way I turned, it was there, and the same distance away. Our house then, was in the centre of the world. It grew upon me that I ought to walk out to the horizon and see what the end of the world was like. The daring of the thing held me back for a while, but the thing became so urgent that I showed it to my friend, Carrie Roberts, and asked her to go with me. She agreed. We sat up in the trees and disputed about what the end of the world would be like when we got there – whether it was sort of tucked under like the hem of a dress, or just was a sharp drop off into nothingness. So we planned to slip off from our folks bright and soon next morning and go see.

   I could hardly sleep that night from the excitement of the thing. I had been yearning for so many months to find out about the end of things. I had no doubts about the beginnings. They were somewhere in the five acres that was home to me. Most likely in Mama's room. Now, I was going to see the end, and then I would be satisfied.

   As soon as breakfast was over, I sneaked off to the meeting place in the scrub palmettoes, a short way from our house and waited. Carrie didn't come

Part One—Genre

right away. I was on my way to her house by a round-about way when I met her. She was coming to tell me that she couldn't go. It looked so far that maybe we wouldn't get back by sundown, and then we would both get a whipping. When we got big enough to wear long dresses, we could go and stay as long as we wanted to. Nobody couldn't whip us then. No matter how hard I begged, she wouldn't go. The thing was too bold and brazen to her thinking. We had a fight, then. I had to hit Carrie to keep my heart from stifling me. Then I was sorry I had struck my friend, and went on home and hid under the house with my heartbreak. But I did not give up the idea of my journey. I was merely lonesome for someone brave enough to undertake it with me. I wanted it to be Carrie. She was a lot of fun, and always did what I told her. Well, most of the time, she did. This time it was too much for even her loyalty to surmount. She even tried to talk me out of my trip. I couldn't give up. It meant too much to me. I decided to put it off until I had something to ride on, then I could go by myself.

So for weeks I saw myself sitting astride of a fine horse. My shoes had sky-blue bottoms to them, and I was riding off to look at the belly-band of the world.

It was summer time, and the mockingbirds sang all night long in the orange trees. Alligators trumpeted from their stronghold in Lake Belle. So fall passed and then it was Christmas time.

Papa did something different a few days before Christmas. He sort of shoved back from the table after dinner and asked us all what we wanted Santa Claus to bring us. My big brothers wanted a baseball outfit. Ben and Joel wanted air rifles. My sister wanted patent leather pumps and a belt. Then it was my turn. Suddenly a beautiful vision came before me. Two things could work together. My Christmas present could take me to the end of the world.

'I want a fine black riding horse with white leather saddle and bridles,' I told Papa happily.

'You, what?' Papa gasped. 'What was dat you said?'

'I said, I want a black saddle horse with . . .'

'A saddle horse!' Papa exploded. 'It's a sin and a shame! Lemme tell you something right now, my young lady; you ain't white.* Riding horse! Always trying to wear de big hat! I don't know how you got in this family nohow. You ain't like none of de rest of my young 'uns.'

'If I can't have no riding horse, I don't want nothing at all,' I said stubbornly with my mouth, but inside I was sucking sorrow. My longed-for journey looked impossible.

---

* That is a Negro saying that means "Don't be too ambitious. You are a Negro and they are not meant to have but so much".

My life

'I'll riding-horse you, Madam!' Papa shouted and jumped to his feet. But being down at the end of the table big enough for all ten members of the family together, I was near the kitchen door, and I beat Papa to it by a safe margin. He chased me as far as the side gate and turned back. So I did not get my horse to ride off to the edge of the world. I got a doll for Christmas.

Since Papa would not buy me a saddle horse, I made me one up. No one around me knew how often I rode my prancing horse, nor the things I saw in far places. Jake, my puppy, always went along and we made great admiration together over the things we saw and ate. We both agreed that it was nice to be always eating things.

Zora Neale Hurston, *Dust Tracks on a Road*

Talking points

- Later in her life, the author of this extract became an anthropologist (someone who studies human behaviour) and famous novelist. Is there anything in this extract that would lead you to guess that she would be a writer and scientist in later life?

- What do you think of her father's attitude? Why does he get so angry when she asks for the horse?

- Why do you think Carrie decides not to go with Zora?

- What does the ending tell us about the author's character? If she had been given a horse for Christmas, would that have satisfied her?

- What does the black riding horse stand for in the author's mind? In your pair or group, write down five to ten words you associate with the image of a prancing black horse with white leather saddle and bridles.

- What lesson do you think this episode seems to have taught the author?

Part One—Genre

Suggestions for writing

1 Write about a dream world you had as a child, where you were free to have adventures. Perhaps you invented one with your friends. If so, explain the games you used to play.

2 Write about a time when you argued with a friend. Describe the events that led up to the argument and how it was finally sorted out.

3 Write a children's story (aimed at four to six year olds), using the idea of a girl riding off on a horse to find the edge of the world as your starting point. You will need to illustrate your story and make sure that the language is simple and clear enough for a young child to read. How will your story end? Will the girl find the edge of the world – or something else?

Books and Me

This unit is about early reading and the memories that surround it. The books that we read as very young children remain in our memories long into adulthood, and many writers look back on their first reading experience with great tenderness.

Part One–Genre

Talking points

In a group, think of all the books that you remember reading in junior school. Go back as far as you can, including reading-scheme books and books that were read to you before you were able to read them yourself. Take a large piece of sugar-paper and write down as many titles as you can remember. When you have filled the paper, circle any titles that have been read by more than one member of your group.

Now report back to the class. Explain which were the most popular books, and talk about any books that were particularly loved or hated by someone in your group. When every group has reported back to the class, think about the following questions:

- Which were the most popular books or authors?

- Were there many books that you had heard of, even if you have not read them?

- Were any non-fiction books mentioned?

- Was there a pattern to most people's reading history? For example, did people stick to reading one particular author or type of book for a time and then move on?

- Did everyone learn to read through a reading scheme?

- Did most people have happy memories of their early encounters with books?

- Did anyone read series of books like 'Sweet Valley High' or 'Point Horror'?

When you have finished your discussion, write a brief account of your findings. Do not write about your own experiences – that will come later.

Memories of early reading

In the following extracts, four writers describe their earliest memories of books. You will see that these memories are very much connected in the writers' minds with the relationships they had with their parents. As they all became writers in later life, it is natural that these authors look back fondly on memories, as being their first steps towards a writing career.

Books

Before I could read, almost a baby, I imagined that God, this strange thing or person I heard about, was a book. Sometimes it was a large book standing upright and half open and I could see the print inside but it made no sense to me. Other times the book was smaller and inside were sharp flashing things. The smaller book was, I am sure now, my mother's needle-book, and the sharp flashing things were her needles with the sun on them.

I was so slow learning to read that my parents had become worried about me. Then suddenly, with a leap as it were, I could manage quite long words. Soon I could make sense of the fairy stories Irish Granny sent – the red, the blue, the green, the yellow. Then she sent *The Heroes*, *The Adventures of Ulysses*, *Perseus and Andromeda*. I read everything I could get hold of. There was the usual glassed-in bookcase at the end of the sitting-room, but it was never locked, the key was lost, and the only warning was that we must keep it shut, for the books must be protected against insects.

I can still see the volumes of the *Encyclopaedia Britannica* that I never touched, a large Bible and several history books, yellow-backed novels and on the top shelf a rather odd selection of poets, Milton, Byron, then Crabbe, Cowper, Mrs Hemans, also *Robinson Crusoe*, *Treasure Island*, *Gulliver's Travels*, *Pilgrim's Progress*.

My nurse, who was called Meta, didn't like me much anyway, and complete with a book it was too much. One day she found me crouched on the staircase reading a bowdlerised* version of the *Arabian Nights* in very small print.

She said, 'If all you read so much, you know what will happen to you? Your eyes will drop out and they will look at you from the page.'

'If my eyes dropped out I wouldn't see,' I argued.

She said, 'They drop out except the little black points you see with.'

I half believed her and imagined my pupils like heads of black pins and all the rest gone. But I went on reading.

Jean Rhys, *Smile Please*

---

*bowdlerised means that all references to sex were removed.

Part One—Genre

Nicholas Nickleby

'Here's a big fat book for you, son. It's by old Charlie Dickens. He hadn't been long gone from the world when I was just a nipper.'

It was a very fat book, the fattest I had ever seen, fatter even than the Bible.

' "That will do for my boy," I said to the woman who was throwing it out. "He'll put it to good use." '

The book my father had rescued for me was *Nicholas Nickleby*. It smelt mouldy, and its pages had turned yellow.

'Don't turn your nose up at it, son. I know it's seen better days, but the words are the same ones Charlie wrote, and that's what matters.'

I placed *Nicholas Nickleby* on the kitchen table, because it was far too heavy to hold. I studied every one of the drawings inside, in the order they appeared – starting with 'Mr Ralph Nickleby's First Visit to his Poor Relations' and ending with 'The Children at their Cousin's Grave'. Mr Ralph Nickleby seemed to be very angry at having to visit his poor relations, who didn't look at all poor to me – the women had on long dresses that weren't torn, and the man was quite smart in his funny coat with the two bits hanging down the back that my father told me were called 'tails'. I didn't think they looked as poor as the gypsies on the other side of the street, who went off to Kent for their holidays to pick hops.

'There's poor, and then there's poor,' said my mother, from the stove. 'If I've told you once, I've told you a thousand times – being poor doesn't mean being scruffy. Don't judge people by the likes of *them*.'

I asked my father if Nicholas was real.

'No, son. He'd be make-believe, wouldn't he? Out of Charlie's head.'

That evening, when supper was over and the dishes washed, my father and I were banished to the front room. He had promised to read to me from the 'dust trap', and my mother wanted to listen to some nice music on the wireless.

He began at the beginning.

' "There once lived, in a —" '

He cleared his throat, and began again.

' "There once lived, in a —" ' He gulped. ' "— in Devonshire, one Mr Godfrey Nickleby . . ." '

(Four years after his death, when I put *Nicholas Nickleby* to the 'good use' he had predicted, I realized why he had cleared his throat, why he had gulped, why he had been embarrassed – it was the word 'sequestered' in the novel's opening sentence: 'There once lived, in a sequestered part of the county of Devonshire, one Mr Godfrey Nickleby . . .' 'Sequestered' was totally foreign to him. He'd never had cause to say 'sequestered'. The sight of it on the page had upset him, briefly; had made him keenly aware of his ignorance. The cough and the gulp were his camouflage for that hated 'sequestered'.)

Books and me

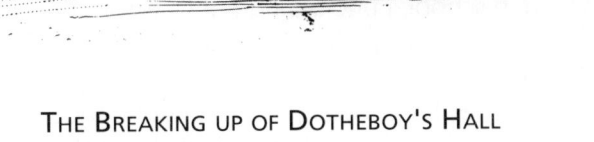

THE BREAKING UP OF DOTHEBOY'S HALL

Part One—Genre

My mother disapproved of *Nicholas Nickleby*. It was a book with a Past — it had been in other hands, and God alone knew whose hands they were. It was old, and it gave off a nasty smell. Its days, in her view, were numbered.

'I can't think what possessed your father to bring it into the house.'

'He brought it home for me.'

'Then why don't you repay him and read it, instead of leaving it about the place to gather dust?'

'I will read it. One day.'

I was fifteen when the day came. I opened *Nicholas Nickleby*, and closed it shut within the hour.

'I have some good news for you,' I told my mother.

'Your good news is usually my bad. What is it now?'

'You can throw this away.' I handed her the 'dust trap'.

'I shall do no such thing. Your father brought that home for you.'

'I'm going to have to borrow it from the library,' I said teasing her. Then I explained why. 'There are pages missing. Dozens of them.'

'Your dad was not to know.' The sharpness had left her voice. 'The woman didn't say. He thought it would make you happy. He wasn't to know it wouldn't.'

(Watching *Nicholas Nickleby* in the theatre, in 1980, when I was forty-three, I found myself in tears. I remembered my father giving me the book, I remembered 'sequestered', I remembered rushing off to the library on Lavender Hill to get another, complete, copy, and the joy of finding one on the shelves.)

Paul Bailey, *An Immaculate Mistake*

Books and Father

A few months after I started school, a thing solemn and exciting happened, which determined my entire life after that. Father brought home a book for me. He took me alone into a back room, where we children slept, and explained it to me. It was *The Arabian Nights*, in an edition for children. There was a colourful picture on the cover, I think it was Aladdin and his magic lamp. My father spoke very earnestly and encouragingly to me and told me how nice it would be to read. He read me a story, saying that all the other stories in the book were as lovely as this one, and that I should try to read them and then in the evening always tell him what I had read. Once I'd finished the book, he'd bring me another. I didn't have to be told twice, and even though I had only just learned how to read in school, I pitched right into the wondrous book and had something to report to him every evening. He kept his promise, there was always a new book there; I never had to skip a single day of reading.

The books were a series for children, all in the same square format. They differed only in the colourful picture on the cover. The letters were the same size in all volumes, it was like reading the same book on and on. But what a series that was, it has never had its peer. I can remember all the titles. After *The Arabian Nights* came Grimm's fairy tales, *Robinson Crusoe*, *Gulliver's Travels*, *Tales from Shakespeare*, *Don Quijote*, Dante, *William Tell*. I wonder how it was possible to adapt Dante for children. Every volume had several gaudy pictures, but I didn't like them, the stories were a lot more beautiful; I don't even know whether I would recognize the pictures today. It would be easy to show that almost everything that I consisted of later on was already in these books, which I read for my father in the seventh year of my life. Of the characters who never stopped haunting me after that, only Odysseus was missing.

I spoke about each book to my father after reading it. Sometimes I was so excited that he had to calm me down. But he never told me, as adults will, that fairy tales are untrue; I am particularly grateful to him for that, perhaps I still consider them true today. I noticed, of course, that Robinson Crusoe was different from Sinbad the Sailor, but it never occurred to me to think less of one of these stories than the other. However, I did have bad dreams about Dante's Inferno. When I heard my mother say to him, 'Jacques, you shouldn't have given him that, it's too early for him,' I was afraid he wouldn't bring me any more books, and I learned to keep my dreams a secret.

Elias Canetti, *The Tongue Set Free*

Part One—Genre

Harry the Hedgehog

When he got home in the evening my father always read to me before I went to bed. My mother also read to me during the day, and together we listened to the story on 'Listen with Mother', and later I joined her for the story on 'Woman's Hour'. No matter that I could not understand it. I loved the words.

Books and me

My father bought me a lot of books, and I quickly knew them by heart, we read them so frequently. If my mother tried to skip a page, I knew instantly and made her go back and read the thing through in full. Reading was not just a matter of finding out what happened in a story; it was a ritual. It was the words that mattered. The characters of the books became realities to me when I played alone. I had endless conversations with Little Grey Rabbit and her *ménage*. There was one book that was a special favourite. It concerned a hedgehog called Harry, and featured human beings as creatures called 'mortals'. I can't remember much about the story, but the word 'mortal', once I knew what it meant, coloured the rather sombre story for me with melancholy. Whenever my mother or Meachey* offered to read to me I produced *Harry the Hedgehog* till they both got heartily sick of it. But it was no use offering me anything else. Nothing else would do. My mother thought the book was morbid and quietly disposed of it. I noticed its absence and guessed what had happened. It was no use complaining. Adults were omnipotent, and I mourned the lost book, trying to recapture the beautiful sadness as best I could. I bided my time.

One day, when my grandmother was staying with us, she took me on the village bus into a nearby market-town for tea. We did some shopping and she offered to buy me a book, which was the best present I could have. In the children's department I scoured the shelves with eagle eye. I knew exactly what I was looking for. Granny offered me one or two books, but I shook my head. At last I saw it. I couldn't read, but I recognized Harry himself on the cover.

'That one!' I cried.

Granny looked at it.

'*Harry the Hedgehog?*' she read. I nodded firmly.

'Are you sure that's the one you want, dear?' She was puzzled by my insistence but finally agreed.

My mother and Meachey were having a cup of tea when we returned. I tried not to look too triumphant. I wanted to be generous in my victory.

'Granny's bought me a new book!' I said, cuddling up to my mother with a winning smile.

'Aren't you a lucky girl! Say "Thank you" to Granny!'

'I already have,' I answered truthfully and produced my parcel. 'Look, Meachey!' I said, innocently.

She looked. 'Oh, no!' she wailed. 'Oh, my God! Not *Harry the Hedgehog*! Oh, Mrs Armstrong! I can't stand it!'

'It *was* a pity we lost the old one,' I said sweetly. 'Isn't it kind of Granny! Let's have it tonight.'

Karen Armstrong, *Through the Narrow Gate*

---

*Mrs Meacham, the housekeeper.

Part One–Genre

makes all sorts of laudable resolutions; he will do exercises every morning and learn a foreign language, and he simply won't let his spirit be broken. He dusts his suit and continues his voyage of exploration round his puny realm – five paces long by four paces broad. He tries the iron bedstead. The springs are broken, the wire mattress sags and cuts into the flesh; it's like lying in a hammock made of steel wire. He pulls a face, being determined to prove that he is full of courage and confidence. Then his gaze rests on the cell door, and he sees that an eye is glued to the spy-hole and is watching him.

The eye goggles at him glassily, its pupil unbelievably big; it is an eye without a man attached to it, and for a few moments the prisoner's heart stops beating.

The eye disappears and the prisoner takes a deep breath and presses his hand against the left side of his chest.

'Now, then,' he says to himself encouragingly, 'how silly to go and get so

It was like this

frightened. You must get used to that; after all, the official's only doing his duty by peeping in; that's part of being in prison. But they won't get me down, they'll never get me down; I'll stuff paper in the spy-hole at night. . . .'

As a matter of fact there's no reason why he shouldn't do so straight away. The idea fills him with genuine enthusiasm. For the first time he experiences that almost maniac desire for activity that from now on will alternate continually – up and down in a never-ending zig-zag – with melancholia and depression.

Then he realises that he has no paper on him, and his next impulse is – according to his social status – either to ring or to run over to the stationer's at the corner. This impulse lasts only the fraction of a second; the next moment he becomes conscious for the first time of the true significance of his situation. For the first time he grasps the full reality of being behind a door which is locked from outside, grasps it in all its searing, devastating poignancy.

This, too, lasts only a few seconds. The next moment the anaesthetising mechanism gets going again, and brings about that merciful state of semi-narcosis induced by pacing up and down, forging plans, weaving illusions.

'Let's see,' says the novice, 'where were we? Ah, yes, that business of stuffing paper in the spy-hole. It *must* be possible to get hold of paper somehow or other.' He leaves the 'how' in this 'somehow' suspended in mid-air. This is a mode of thought that he will soon master – or, rather, it will master him. 'When I get out,' he will say for example, 'I shall never worry about money again. I shall rub along somehow or other.' Or: 'When I get out, I shall never quarrel with the wife again. We'll manage to get along somehow.'

Indeed, 'somehow or other' everything will be all right once he's free.

The fact that the prisoner follows this stereotyped line of thought, which, as I say, is going, after a few days, completely to master him, means that the outside world increasingly loses its reality for him; it becomes a dream world in which everything is somehow or other possible.

'Where were we? . . . Oh, yes, that business of stuffing paper in the spy-hole. Of course, somehow or other one can get hold of some paper. But is it allowed? No, it's certain not to be allowed. So why bother? . . .

'Let's take a more thorough inventory of the objects in the room. Why, look, there's an iron table with a chair which we haven't observed or fully appreciated yet. Of course the chair can't be moved from the table; it's welded to it. A pity, otherwise one might use it as a bed table and put one's things on it when getting undressed – pocket-book*, handkerchief, cigarettes, matches and so on ...'

Then it occurs to him that he has neither pocket-book nor handkerchief, cigarettes nor matches in his pocket.

The barometer of his mood falls a second time.

It rises again the moment he has tried the tap over the wash-basin. Look,

---

* wallet

43

there's running water in prison – it isn't half as bad as one imagined from outside. After all, there is a bed (and it's much healthier to sleep on a hard bed), a washbasin, a table, a chair – what more does a man need? One must learn to live simply and unassumingly: a few exercises, reading, writing, learning a foreign language . . .'

The next voyage of discovery is in the direction of the water closet. 'Why, there's even one of these – it's really not half so bad.' He pulls the plug. The chain refuses to function. And the barometer falls afresh.

It rises again once the subtle plan has been conceived of filling the bucket with water from the tap and of flushing the lavatory pan in this way. It falls again when it transpires that the tap has also ceased to function. It rises again when he reflects that there must be certain times of the day when the water runs. It falls – it rises – it falls – it rises. And this is how things are to go on – in the coming minutes, hours, days, weeks, years.

How long has he already been in the cell?

He looks at his watch: exactly three minutes.

Arthur Koestler, *Dialogue with Death*

Talking points

- How does this real-life account compare to the one you wrote about or imagined?

- Why do you think the author writes about his own experiences in the third person ('he') instead of in the first person ('I')?

- This is not an obviously horrifying account of being in a prison cell, there are no rats or rusty chains. What is it, then, that makes this extract so disturbing?

Wounded

In Spain in 1937 George Orwell was shot by a sniper. In this extract he explains what it felt like.

I had been about ten days at the front when it happened. The whole experience of being hit by a bullet is very interesting and I think it is worth describing in detail.

It was at the corner of the parapet, at five o'clock in the morning. This was always a dangerous time, because we had the dawn at our backs, and if you stuck your head above the parapet it was clearly outlined against the sky. I was talking to the sentries preparatory to changing the guard. Suddenly, in the very

It was like this

middle of saying something, I felt – it is very hard to describe what I felt, though I remember it with the utmost vividness.

Roughly speaking it was the sensation of being *at the centre* of an explosion. There seemed to be a loud bang and a blinding flash of light all round me, and I felt a tremendous shock – no pain, only a violent shock, such as you get from an electric terminal; with it a sense of utter weakness, a feeling of being stricken and shrivelled up to nothing. The sandbags in front of me receded into immense distance. I fancy you would feel much the same if you were struck by lightning. I knew immediately that I was hit, but because of the seeming bang and flash I thought it was a rifle nearby that had gone off accidentally and shot me. All this happened in a space of time much less than a second. The next moment my knees crumpled up and I was falling, my head hitting the ground with a violent bang which, to my relief, did not hurt. I had a numb, dazed feeling, a consciousness of being very badly hurt, but no pain in the ordinary sense.

Part One—Genre

The American sentry I had been talking to had started forward. 'Gosh! Are you hit?' People gathered round. There was the usual fuss – 'Lift him up! Where's he hit? Get his shirt open!' etc., etc. The American called for a knife to cut my shirt open. I knew that there was one in my pocket and tried to get it out, but discovered that my right arm was paralysed. Not being in pain, I felt a vague satisfaction. This ought to please my wife, I thought; she had always wanted me to be wounded, which would save me from being killed when the great battle came. It was only now that it occurred to me to wonder where I was hit, and how badly; I could feel nothing, but I was conscious that the bullet had struck me somewhere in the front of my body. When I tried to speak I found that I had no voice, only a faint squeak, but at the second attempt I managed to ask where I was hit. In the throat, they said, Harry Webb, our stretcher-bearer, had brought a bandage and one of the little bottles of alcohol they gave us for field-dressings. As they lifted me up a lot of blood poured out my mouth, and I heard a Spaniard behind me say that the bullet had gone clear through my neck. I felt the alcohol, which at ordinary times would sting like the devil, splash on to the wound as a pleasant coolness.

They laid me down again while somebody fetched a stretcher. As soon as I knew that the bullet had gone clean through my neck I took it for granted that I was done for. I had never heard of a man or an animal getting a bullet through the middle of the neck and surviving it. The blood was dribbling out of the corner of my mouth. 'The artery's gone,' I thought. I wondered how long you last when your carotid artery is cut; not many minutes, presumably. Everything was very blurry. There must have been about two minutes during which I assumed that I was killed. And that too was interesting – I mean it is interesting to know what your thoughts would be at such a time. My first thought, conventionally enough, was for my wife. My second was a violent resentment at having to leave this world which, when all is said and done, suits me so well. I had time to feel this very vividly. The stupid mischance infuriated me. The meaninglessness of it! To be bumped off, not even in battle, but in this stale corner of the trenches, thanks to a moment's carelessness! I thought, too, of the man who had shot me – wondered what he was like, whether he was a Spaniard or a foreigner, whether he knew he had got me, and so forth. I could not feel any resentment against him. I reflected that as he was a Fascist I would have killed him if I could, but that if he had been taken prisoner and brought before me at this moment I would merely have congratulated him on his good shooting. It may be, though, that if you were really dying your thoughts would be quite different.

They had just got me on to the stretcher when my paralysed right arm came to life and began hurting damnably. At the time I imagined that I must have broken it in falling; but the pain reassured me, for I knew that your sensations do not become more acute when you are dying. I began to feel more normal and to be sorry for the four poor devils who were sweating and slithering with the stretcher on their shoulders. It was a mile and a half to the ambulance, and vile going, over lumpy, slippery tracks. I knew what a sweat it was, having helped to carry a wounded man down a day or two earlier. The leaves of the silver poplars which, in places, fringed our trenches brushed against my face; I thought what a good thing it was to be alive in a world where silver poplars grow. But all the while the pain in my arm was diabolical, making me swear and then try not to swear, because every time I breathed too hard the blood bubbled out of my mouth.

George Orwell, *Homage to Catalonia*

Talking points

- Here is a list of words which could be used to describe the author's feelings from the moment he is shot to the moment he is taken to hospital on the stretcher:

puzzled	resigned	numb	glad
shocked	sad	dazed	resentful
confused	surprised		relieved

  Put the words in the order in which the author feels them. You may use words twice or add any of your own if you think you need to.
  When you are satisfied, compare your list with another group's.

- Koestler takes us through an experience of discovery, hope and disappointment in what turns out only to have been three minutes. Orwell describes all the thoughts and feelings that went through his mind in the moments after being shot. Our perception of time alters depending on our situation. Sometimes a minute seems like an eternity.

  Have there been times in your life when time seems to have stood still?

  Working with a partner or in a small group, try to describe something that happened to you. How did you feel? What were the thoughts that went through your head?

  Here are some possibilities:
  - The night before Christmas (or a birthday)
  - An accident
  - In the dentist's waiting room

Part One–Genre

- Running a race
- Waiting for test results to be read out
- Waiting to be seen by a teacher when you are in trouble
- Being in a fight
- A disappointment
- The night before going on holiday.

Try to explain your thoughts and feelings as honestly as you can.

Suggestion for writing

Take the experience you have described in the exercise above and transfer your description to paper. You could follow this plan.

a) Write down all the feelings you experienced. Sort them out into the right order.

b) Write down all the thoughts that went through your mind during your experience. Write them as if you were speaking them aloud.

c) Now combine the thoughts and feelings into a single piece of writing.

Remember, your piece of writing does not have to be long, but it must be as accurate and vivid as possible.

(If there is nothing in your own experience that comes to mind, you could write a fictional account instead.)

It was like this

Lepelstraat

Jewish writer Marga Minco was a schoolgirl in 1940 when Nazi Germany invaded her native Holland. Her family was arrested and later died in concentration camps. She survived to tell us what it was like to be alive in those times.

In this extract, she describes what happened to her one day when her mother sent her out to do some shopping.

As I entered Lepelstraat I saw a truck approaching at the end of the street. Men wearing steel helmets and green uniforms were sitting erect behind each other on the seats. The vehicle stopped and the men jumped out. I turned round and wanted to walk back, but another truck had already driven into the street from the other end, behind me. In that one, too, the men were sitting immobile and bolt upright, rifles between their knees, like tin soldiers in a toy car. They all jumped down at the same time, on both sides, went up to the houses and pushed open the doors. Most of them were already ajar, and so they were able to go in without trouble.

One of the soldiers came up to me. He said I had to get into the truck. Nobody was sitting in it.

'I don't live here,' I said.

'Never mind about that – get in,' said the man in the green uniform.

I stood my ground. 'No,' I said again, decidedly. 'I don't live in Lepelstraat. You ask your commandant whether Jewish people living in another street have to go along as well.'

He turned and walked towards the officer in charge, who was watching his subordinates at work from a point some yards away from the truck. They exchanged a few words, in the course of which the soldier pointed towards me once or twice.

I had remained standing at the same spot, and saw a little boy come out of a doorway close by. He had a rucksack in one hand, and a piece of bread and treacle in the other. A brown smear ran down over his chin. From beyond an open door I heard heavy footsteps on the stairs.

The soldier came back and asked for my identity card. He went with it to the officer, who looked at it and gave it back to the soldier. He muttered something; his lips moved. With the identity card in the same hand that grasped the rifle, the soldier came back to me again. He walked more slowly than he had done the first time. He trod on a scrap of paper that blew across the pavement. His helmet began immediately above his eyes; it looked as if his forehead was of green steel. The little boy in the doorway had finished his bread and treacle, and was tying the rucksack on his back.

Part One—Genre

The soldier handed me the identity card and told me I could go. I walked past the truck. A few women were sitting on the benches now. An old woman was climbing awkwardly in. She was carrying a brown blanket. A man behind her pushed her up into the truck. Somewhere, someone pounded hard on a door. A window was banged shut.

In Roetersstraat I began to run fast, and did not stop running until I reached home.

'How quick you've been!' said my mother. 'Haven't you been to the butcher's?'

'No,' I said. 'It wasn't possible.'

'Why? Was he shut?'

'No. Lepelstraat was closed.'

Next morning I walked down Lepelstraat again. It was littered with paper. Doors were standing wide open everywhere. In the dark entrance to an upstairs flat a grey cat was sitting on the steps. When I stopped to look at it, the animal fled up higher and glared down at me from the top, with arched, bristling back. A child's glove was lying on one of the steps.

A few houses farther on a door hung askew, half off its hinges. The panels were splintered and the box for letters on the inside was hanging crookedly from one nail. Some papers were sticking out of it. I could not clearly see whether they were circulars or letters. From various open windows the curtains fluttered out in the wind. On one window frame a flower-pot had fallen over on its side. Through another window I saw a table still laid for a meal. A piece of bread on a plate. A knife stuck into the butter.

The kosher butcher's shop where I was to have bought meat the day before was empty. A plank had been nailed across the door, so that no one could get in. That must have been done quite early on. From outside, the shop looked nice and neat. As if the butcher had cleaned it out thoroughly first.

The roller shutter in front of the pickle merchant's little hall was down. The vinegary smell of the casks of gherkins still hung about it. From under the shutter a wet trail ran across the pavement to the gutter. It must have come from barrels that had fallen over.

Suddenly the wind began to blow. The bits of paper whirled over the asphalt, struck against the houses. Near by, a door slammed shut. No one had come out. A window clattered. No hand was raised to close it. A shutter banged to. But it was not yet night.

Before I turned the corner I saw something on a doorpost. An enamel plate with a red eye, showing that the house was under the protection of the Night Watch Service.

The door was open.

Marga Minco, *Bitter Herbs*

Talking points

- Why do you think that the German soldiers allowed the author to go?

- Why do you think the author did not tell her mother what had happened to her in Lepelstraat?

- There is a dream-like quality to this account of the Jews being taken away to the concentration camps. There is no shouting or fighting, nor even crying. Why do you think some people apparently behaved so calmly?

- Can you find any evidence in the extract to show that not everybody left without a fight?

Part One–Genre

Suggestions for writing

1 Use the poetic style of this extract to make a poem of your own.

Either with a partner or by yourself choose four or five sentences from this extract – some from the beginning, some from the middle and some from the end. Copy them on to a piece of paper and use them to make a poem. You may alter the sentences and add other words of your own if you wish.

You could illustrate your poem to make it more effective.

2 One of the things that makes this extract so sad is the final section in which the author describes Lepelstraat deserted. We know that most of the inhabitants never returned to their shops and homes, so the picture she paints of boarded shops, battered doors and paper all over the street seems all the more desolate.

Imagine a place you know well that is usually full of life – a high street or market, for example.

Now imagine that all the people in this place have been rounded up and taken away.

Write two descriptions: one when the place is crowded, and one after all the people have been taken away.

If you are interested in reading more on this subject, here are some books that deal with the experience of Jewish people during the Second World War:

Friedrich by Hans Peter Richter
Mischling: Second Degree by Ilse Koehn
The Diary of Ann Frank

Travellers' Tales

We all love to visit new and interesting places, but very few of us are able to travel the world. If we can't really travel, then at least we can read about places we may never visit. This unit is devoted to travel writing. In it, writers from various centuries enable us to see strange places through their eyes.

Part One–Genre

Vale Perilous

The first extract is from the fourteenth-century *Travels* of Sir John Mandeville, who was probably the first popular travel writer. However, no one knows if he actually went anywhere or simply made his adventures up!

In this extract he has to make a very tricky decision. Should he go through the Vale Perilous or not?

Before you read the extract, discuss in your groups what the 'Vale Perilous' might be. When you think you have come to some conclusions, read on.

A little way from that place towards the River Phison [Ganges] is a great marvel. For there is a valley between two hills, about four miles long; some men call it the Vale of Enchantment, some the Vale of Devils, and some the Vale Perilous. In this valley there are often heard tempests, and ugly, hideous noises, both by day and by night. And sometimes noises are heard as if of trumpets and tabors and drums, like at the feasts of great lords. This valley is full of devils and always has been, and men of those parts say it is an entrance to Hell. There is much gold and silver in this valley, and to get it many men – Christian and heathen – come and go into that valley. But very few come out again – least of all unbelievers – for all who go therein out of covetousness are strangled by devils and lost. In the middle of the valley under a rock one can clearly see the head and face of a devil, very hideous and dreadful to see; nothing else is seen of it except from the shoulders up. There is no man in this world, Christian or anyone else, who would not be very terrified to see it, it is so horrible and foul. He looks at each man so keenly and so cruelly, and his eyes are rolling so fast and sparkling like fire, and he changes his expression so often, and out of his nose and mouth comes so much fire of different colours with such an awful stench, that no man can bear it. But good Christian men, however, who are firm in the faith, can enter that valley without great harm if they are cleanly confessed and absolved and bless themselves with the sign of the Cross; then devils will not harm them. Even if they do get out without bodily hurt, they will not escape without great fear; for devils appear openly to them, menace them, and fly up and down in the air with great thunders and lightnings and awful tempests. Good men as well as evil will have great fear when they pass through, thinking that perhaps God will take vengeance on them for their past sins. My companions and I, when we came near that valley and heard all about it, wondered in our hearts whether to trust ourselves totally to the mercy of God and pass through it; some turned aside and said they would not put themselves in that danger. There were in our company two Friars Minor of Lombardy, who said they would go through that valley if we would go with them; so what with their encouragement and the comfort of their words, we confessed cleanly and

Travellers' tales

heard Mass and took Communion and went into the valley, fourteen of us together. But when we came out we were only nine. We knew never what became of the remainder, whether they were lost or turned back, but we never saw them again. Two of them were Greeks and three Spaniards. Our other companions, who would not cross the Vale Perilous, went round by another way to meet us. And my companions and I went through the valley, and saw many marvellous things, and gold and silver and precious stones and many other jewels on each side of us – so it seemed to us. But whether it really was as it seemed, or was merely illusion, I do not know. But because of the fear that we were in, and also so as not to hinder our devotion, we would touch nothing we saw: for we were more devout then than we ever were before or after, because of the fear we had on account of devils appearing to us in different guises and of the multitude of dead men's bodies that lay in our path. For if two kings with their armies had fought together and the greater part of both sides been slain, there would not have been a greater number of dead bodies than we saw. And when I saw so many bodies lying there, I was very astonished that they were so healthy, without corruption, as fresh as if they had been newly dead. But I dare not affirm that they were all true bodies that I saw in that valley; I believe that devils made so many bodies appear so as to frighten us; for it is not likely that so great a multitude of folk should have really been dead

Part One—Genre

there so freshly that there was no smell or corruption. Many of those bodies I saw seemed to be wearing the clothing of Christian men; but I well believe they came there from covetousness of the gold and other jewels in that valley, or because false hearts cannot stand the great fear and dread that they had on account of the horrible sights they saw. And I assure you that we were often struck to the earth by terrible great blasts of wind, thunder and tempests; but through the grace of Almighty God we passed through safe and sound.

Sir John Mandeville, Travels

Talking points

- Do you believe this story? If not, what is it that makes it hard to believe? How does the author deal with the possibility that the reader might not believe what he's written?

- Can you think of any episodes from films you have seen or stories that you have read that are similar to this tale?

- In the fourteenth century, readers of travellers' tales did not know what to expect and wanted to believe the most outlandish things. In a way they did not care whether the accounts were truthful or not so long as they were exciting. There is something similar in our fascination with space and aliens today.

The following extract is taken from an interview with Travis Walton, who claims to have been abducted by aliens. According to reports, in 1975 he and his workmates were returning from trimming trees in Snowflake Arizona when a flying saucer came out of the sky and hovered above their truck. Walton climbed out and walked towards the spaceship. There was a blue and white flash, and Walton fell to the ground. The others panicked and fled. When they returned, he was gone and he was not seen again until five days later. He gave this newspaper interview:

Riddle of the vanishing woodsman

'We all saw the saucer that night. I knew what it was right away. When Duane [his brother] was a kid he was followed by a saucer and we promised each other that if it happened again I would not be afraid . . . I just jumped out and ran towards the glow. I felt no fear. I got close and something hit me . . . like an electric blow to my jaw . . . I fell backwards and everything went black . . . When I woke there was a strong light . . . I had problems focussing and pains in my

Travellers' tales

chest and head . . . I was on a table . . . I saw three weird figures . . . not human . . . they looked like well-developed foetuses, about five feet tall, in tan-brown robes, tight-fitting. Their skins were mushroom-white, with no clear features. They made no sound. They had no hair, their foreheads were domed and their eyes very large . . . I panicked . . . jumped up, knocking over a plastic tray . . . I wanted to attack them but they scampered away . . . a man appeared a few feet away . . . human, in helmet and tight-fitting blue uniform . . . he smiled at me and led me through a corridor into another big, bright room . . . a planetarium. Outside it was dark but I recognized some galaxies . . . the man in blue reappeared . . . led me down a ramp, suddenly I was in bright sunlight . . . some kind of hangar. I saw some small space saucers nearby. Then I saw three other people (in helmets). They were human, one a woman, all dressed in blue . . . They took me to a table and eased me on it. They put a mask on my face . . . then things went black again . . . When I woke up I was shaky . . . on the highway. The trees were lit up because their saucer was just a few feet away. I saw nobody . . . I ran until I came to a phone booth. I recognized I was in Heber (a few miles from Snowflake) . . . I phoned my sister, and they came to get me.'

The Fortean Times

Part One—Genre

- Do you believe Walton was telling the truth? If you don't think so, try and work out what made you come to that decision. If you think he *is* telling the truth, try convincing someone else in the class. Are you able to do so?

- Is Walton's story any more or less difficult to believe than Mandeville's?

Suggestions for writing

1 Write a 'traveller's tale' of your own. You could set it in a real but faraway place, or you could invent a place and the people who live there. Try to make it as convincing as you can.
   Here are some ideas to help you:
   - The Lake of Dreams: when you swim in it you dream the most wonderful dreams, but if you stay in too long . . .
   - The Castle of Evil: it's easy to get in, but not so easy to get out.
   - The Tree of Mystery: its fruit is made of gold, but when you climb it . . .

2 Write your own 'Abducted by Aliens' newspaper story. Make sure you include an interview and eyewitness accounts.

Travellers' tales

The marabout's saliva

In this extract from his book, *The Voices of Marrakesh*, Elias Canetti describes an encounter with a blind beggar. This, however, is no ordinary beggar. He appears to be *chewing* money!

I had turned away from the group of eight blind beggars, their litany still in my ear, and gone only a few steps farther when my attention was caught by a white-haired old man standing quite alone with his legs slightly apart; he held his head a little on one side and he was chewing. He too was blind and, to judge from the rags he was dressed in, a beggar. But his cheeks were full and red, his lips healthy and moist. He was chewing slowly with his mouth closed and the expression on his face was a cheerful one. He chewed thoroughly, as if following instructions. It evidently gave him much pleasure, and watching him I was put in mind of his saliva and the fact that he must have a great deal of it. He was standing in front of a row of stalls on which mountains of oranges were banked up for sale; I said to myself that one of the stall-keepers must have given him an orange and that he was chewing that. His right hand stood a little way away from his body. The fingers of that hand were all widely splayed. It looked as if they were paralysed and he could not close them.

There was quite a lot of free space around the old man, which in this busy spot I found surprising. He gave the impression that he was always alone and did not wish it otherwise. I resolutely watched him chewing, intending to wait and see what happened when he had finished. It took a very long time; I had never seen a man chew so heartily and so exhaustively. I felt my own mouth begin to move slightly although it contained nothing that it could have chewed. I experienced something akin to awe at his enjoyment, which struck me as being more conspicuous than anything I had ever seen in association with a human mouth. His blindness failed to fill me with compassion. He seemed collected and content. Not *once* did he interrupt himself to ask for alms as the others all did. Perhaps he had what he wanted. Perhaps he did not need anything else.

When he had finished he licked his lips a few times; stretched his right hand with the splayed fingers a little farther forward, and in a hoarse voice said his piece. I went up to him rather shyly and laid a coin on his palm. The fingers remained stretched; he really could not close them. Slowly he raised the hand towards his face. He pressed the coin to his protruding lips and took it into his mouth. Hardly was it inside before he began chewing again. He pushed the coin this way and that in his mouth and it seemed to me I could follow its movements: now it was on the left, now on the right, and he was chewing as exhaustively as before.

I was amazed and I was dubious. I wondered whether I was not mistaken.

59

Part One—Genre

Perhaps the coin had meanwhile disappeared somewhere else and I had not noticed. I waited again. When he had chewed with the same enjoyment and was finished, the coin appeared between his lips. He spat it into his left hand, which he had raised. A great deal of saliva streamed out with it. Then he slipped the coin into a pouch that he wore on his left.

I tried to dissolve my disgust at this proceeding in its outlandishness. What could be filthier than money? But this old man was not I; what caused me disgust gave him enjoyment, and had I not sometimes seen people kissing coins? The copious saliva undoubtedly had a role to play here, and he was clearly distinguished from other beggars by his ample generation of saliva. He had put in long practice before ever asking for alms; whatever he had eaten before, no one else would have taken so long over it. There was some kind of meaning in the motions of his mouth.

Or had he only taken *my* coin in his mouth? Had he felt in the palm of his hand that it was of a higher denomination than he was usually given and wanted to express his special thanks? I waited to see what would happen next, and I did not find waiting difficult. I was bewildered and intrigued and would certainly not have been able to give my attention to anything but the old man. He repeated his formula a few times. An Arab came past and laid a much smaller coin on his palm. He lifted it to his mouth without hesitating, put it in, and began chewing exactly as before. Possibly he did not chew quite as long this time. He spat the coin out, again with a great deal of saliva, and slipped it into his pouch. He was given other coins, some of them quite small, and the same proceeding was repeated several times. I became more and more perplexed; the longer I looked on, the less I understood why he did it. But one thing there was no doubting any more: he always did it, it was his habit, his particular way of begging, and the people who gave him something expected this expression of interest on the part of his mouth, which seemed to me redder every time he opened it.

I did not notice that people were also looking at me, and I must have presented a ridiculous spectacle. Possibly, who knows, I was even gaping open-mouthed. Then suddenly a man came out from behind his oranges, took a few steps towards me, and said soothingly: 'That's a marabout.' I knew that marabouts were holy men and that special powers were attributed to them. The word aroused awe in me and I felt my disgust immediately dwindle. I asked diffidently: 'But why does he put the coins in his mouth?' 'He always does that,' said the man, as if it had been the most natural thing in the world. He turned away from me and resumed his post behind his oranges. Only now did I notice that behind every stall there were two or three pairs of eyes trained on me. The astonishing creature was myself, who stood so long uncomprehending.

With this information I felt I had been dismissed and stayed no longer. The marabout is a holy man, I told myself, and everything about this holy man is holy, even his saliva. In bringing the givers' coins in contact with his saliva he confers a special blessing on them and thus enhances the merit they have acquired in heaven through their almsgiving. He was sure of paradise, and himself had something to give away that men needed much more than he needed their coins. Now I understood the cheerfulness that was in his blind face and that distinguished him from the other beggars I had seen hitherto.

I went away, but with him so much in mind that I talked about him to all my friends. None of them had ever noticed him and I sensed that they doubted the truth of my words. The next day I went back to the same spot but he was not there. I looked everywhere; he was not to be found. I looked every day; he did not come again. Perhaps he lived alone somewhere in the mountains and only rarely came to the city. I could have asked the orange vendors about him but I was ashamed to face them. He did not mean the same to them as he did to me, and whereas I was not in the least averse to talking about him to friends who had never seen him I tried to keep him separate from people who knew him well and to whom he was a familiar and natural figure. He knew nothing of me and they might perhaps have talked to him about me.

I saw him once more, exactly a week later, again on a Saturday evening. He was standing in front of the same stall, but he had nothing in his mouth and was not chewing. He said his piece. I gave him a coin and waited to see what would happen to it. He was soon chewing it assiduously again, but while he was still busy doing so a man came up to me and said his nonsense: 'That's a marabout. He's blind. He puts the coin in his mouth to feel how much you've given him.' Then he said something to the marabout in Arabic and pointed to me. The old man, his chewing finished, had spat the coin out again. He turned to me, his face shining. He said a blessing for me, which he repeated six times. The friendliness and warmth that passed across to me as he spoke were such as I had never had a person bestow on me before.

Elias Canetti, *The Voices of Marrakesh*

Part One—Genre

Talking points

- The author is obviously embarrassed by his interest in the beggar. Why do you think this?

- What impression do you get of the beggar from this description? Here are some words to help you decide. Which of them apply to the beggar?

    dirty   respected   happy   dignified   calm

    revolting   good   hated   ugly   holy   disabled   mysterious

    friendly   frightening   powerful   weak   pitiful

How does the marabout compare with your idea of what beggars are like?

Suggestions for writing

When the author asks the local trader why the marabout puts the coins in his mouth, he replies 'He always does that'. To the locals, the blind beggar is not unusual; he just blends into the background. Those of us who live in towns and cities are so used to beggars, tramps and buskers on the streets that we simply accept them as part of the scenery. We no longer notice them.

Here are some ideas to explore in writing:

1 Write the thoughts of a beggar or busker as he or she watches the well-off shoppers walk past on the high street.

2 Tell the life story of a tramp, as if you were the tramp. How did he or she come to be living rough? You could imagine the tramp telling his or her life story to someone on a park bench.

Travellers' tales

A Kirghiz dinner

One of the most interesting aspects of travel is eating new and unusual food. In 1932, Ella Maillart, an explorer, writer and actress, travelled through Russian Turkestan by herself. In this extract, she describes a dinner that she found both fascinating and filling.

The old mother takes some of the broth in a ladle, pours it into a bowl, and tastes. Is it strong enough? She passes it to the head man, who considers it satisfactory. Then a child takes a jug of warm water from near the fire and goes round, pouring it on our hands. These latter are held well forward to make sure the water falls into the zone of dead ashes. Then a towel is passed round, the state of which had better be left undescribed, and a light cloth is unfolded in front of the seat of honour to serve as the tablecloth.

Then from the cauldron out comes the liver, which is cut into slices, in addition to chunks of fat – all their sheep have fat tails – and the table is laid. The meal is eaten with the fingers, by making small sandwiches of liver and fat which are plunged into a bowl containing salt passed from hand to hand. The delicate flavour is delicious: I would willingly have made it my main sustenance.

The woman then takes the pieces of meat from the cauldron and begins to sort them out, the head and joints going into a wooden platter, which is passed to Auguste, who is still too ill to be able to eat any. Whereupon our host takes up the head, gouges the eyes out, and eats the points of the ears on the end of his knife. After this the platter is passed to us. The meat is delicious, and comes away of itself from the bone, so tender and succulent, that even when we are full we go on energetically chewing for the pleasure of having the feel of the firm, sweet-tasting flesh in our months.

When I come to a stop at last, my knife, cheeks, and all ten fingers swimming in grease, I begin to observe my Kirghiz neighbours. They are still eating, slowly and scrupulously; masticating the very tendons even. One would think they had not had a decent meal for ages. But, as Karutz writes, 'To realise how they give themselves up to the pleasure of eating, one must have witnessed it oneself. Anybody who wants to know how the mounds composed of the débris of past feasts built themselves up in prehistoric caves, needs only to eat one sheep among the Kirghiz people. He will then realise what a "clean sweep" really means. Only then will he divine the zeal, the understanding, and success with which a mutton bone can be handled, the persistent and ingenious art with which it can be gnawed, scraped, bitten, crushed, broken, sucked; and how without the aid of the least instrument it can be scraped so irreproachably clean.'

When the guests have finished, the dish is passed to the other men, then to the children, and finally to the women.

Part One—Genre

Thus a child can be seen to pass a practically gnawed-clean bone to his father. The gesture might seem ironic, but quite the contrary, for the marrow is considered a great delicacy, and the father sucks mightily away.

The fragments of meat that have come away in the cooking have been put on one side. Now two boys take them, and seizing the meat firmly between the thumb and left forefinger, so that it projects slightly beyond the hand, begin rapidly slicing and, cutting towards themselves, make a hash of it. The fat is treated in the same way, after which a little of the boiling broth is added, and the third course goes round, the 'bish barmak'.

We each help ourselves, filling our bowls, and this, too, is eaten with the fingers, and that needs courage, for if one attempts to grasp the mixture, it is so greasy that it slips away at once, and it is impossible to get a decent mouthful. The Kirghiz are wonderful, for with one hand they take up a handful of the hash, gather it in their palms, and neatly compress it in their shut fingers; then, at the very moment they open their mouths, the fingers are released, so that the food is carried into the lips and sucked up in one breath, leaving the hand absolutely clean.

Try it! It's a trick worthy of a conjuror.

Travellers' tales

Neighbours keep coming in, depositing their goloshes to one side of the doorway before squatting down, and odd relics of the feast are presented to them. For the last course a bowl of broth goes round again, very greasy and hot, because it comes straight out of the cauldron. It does one good. Though I have filled up in every meaning of the term, I drink the velvety, fragrant liquid with delight.

The cloth containing the débris is then gathered up, water is poured over our hands, and the same towel is called into service again. Instinctively I have used the rich white fat that has solidified on my hands to grease my shoes, and lo and behold! our host does the same.

Then everyone stretches out, takes a siesta, and breaks wind. How Matkerim is still able to swallow a few more bowls of koumiss is a mystery to me.

Ella Maillart

Talking points

- Every nation has its own conventions for eating. Can you work out from the extract what the conventions are for the Kirghiz? Compile a list of Kirghiz table manners.

- We are so used to our own table manners that we hardly notice them. In your group, discuss the eating conventions of your family and friends. Here are some questions to help you:
  - Which foods should be eaten with a knife and fork, and which may be eaten with the fingers?
  - What sort of foods are usually eaten at the beginning of a meal? Which are eaten at the end?
  - Who usually gets served first?

  You may find that, if your group consists of people from different cultures, there will be different conventions.

Suggestion for writing

Most people in this country will have tasted Indian or Chinese food, but many people in European countries have not. In Germany or parts of France, for example, you would never find an Indian restaurant.

Write an account of an Indian or Chinese meal that will be read by someone who has never eaten one. Explain, in as much detail as you can, the sort of dishes eaten, how they are eaten, the kind of tastes you would expect, etc.

Part One – Genre

First impressions

One of the great experiences of travelling is seeing a place for the first time. Over the next few pages, you will read three very different first impressions.

In the 1970s Sally Belfrage and her friend Judith gave up their comfortable life in London to join the followers of the guru Rajneesh in Poona, India. An old friend, Dinah, had already joined the sect and has come to meet them. In this extract, Sally Belfrage describes her feelings on arriving in India for the first time and driving through the streets of Bombay.

> Before reading this description of Bombay, think about what pictures the word 'Bombay' brings to your mind. Discuss these with your group and jot down some phrases and words that you agree on.

Bombay

The first view of urban India is surely the worst sight in the world. It can never again be so shocking; one could not survive the repetition of its first assault on the senses. The degradation and the hopeless hordes are so beyond the worst expectations that there is no armour, no protection possible. The first time. But Dinah appears immune next to Judith who is crying, and in a day or two will we not notice either?

Beside me the driver is barefoot. Perhaps it gives him extra sensitivity on the pedals for his hair's-breadth escapes from certain doom, which occur about once a block. It is a wonder he can see, having festooned the car, sun visor to dashboard, with garlands of limp, yesterday's flowers. But blindly or not, he surges through the competition – a choke of pedestrians and cows, bikes and motorbikes, horse- and man-drawn carts, buses and many brightly painted trucks announcing on their rears HORN OK PLEASE – advice adhered to universally. Indeed a child might take the noise for the propellant – we never stop tooting as we overtake whatever's in the way, blast of outrage in return, multiple missings-by-an-inch. It is amazing to be so near disaster and to so barely feel it, because everyone in view is so much nearer a disaster that is more potent still. How can they be alive? So many people! When we stop at a red light (the driver turning off the motor to conserve petrol) they swoop on us crying 'Ma! Ma! Ma!': the skeletal, the blind, tiny children carrying still tinier ones, many with the reddish hair of kwashiorkor, mutilated stumps poking through the window, a vast humiliation grown stoic with need – for when you put a coin in a hand, the hand does not retreat to make room for another, but instantly returns. You have to keep the windows shut against them finally, or they will not let you

Travellers' tales

drive away; then open them quickly for the brief forward sprints or the heat is unendurable.

Like Egypt but more and worse. I never expected to see anything as squalid as Cairo and the amputated limbs of children (the better to beg); as Upper Egypt and the people living in and out of mud, and the trachoma killing the eyes of the villagers there; as the open sewers in a Canton back street in 1957; as the hopeless pueblos of Mexico where nothing is more than a single remove from dust. But this is in another league. If not qualitatively worse off, then quantitatively: with these numbers of people there is so clearly nothing to do. It has gone too far. Billboards bearing slogans suggesting activity and hope make a travesty of a tragedy. INDIA SUCCEEDS AGAINST INFLATION. THE COUNTRY IS ON THE MOVE.

Eccentric details arrest and distract me from the human horror everywhere. A shabby, once grand building is signposted ENGLISH MEDIUM on one side, MARATHI MEDIUM on the other. What can they mean? Voluptuous cinema advertisements display a couple at it on a bed of apples, and other entangled pairs as unlikely to appear on the censored Indian screen but apparently allowed on posters. The faces of the film stars are plump and pink of cheek, a different race of people from the emaciated dark-brown urchin running along next to us heaving with what looks to be his last strength a bus-length cart laden with hardware and bamboo scaffolding. An actual bus, double-decker like the ones in London, is so fully packed that it seems a many-limbed Bosch creature from hell, and the rear platform only just clears the street. Some have their carts pulled by bullocks, with horns lacquered crimson and wearing bells and patchwork coverlets. But most walk, spindly men and women and children bearing burdens three or four times their own bulk on their heads. Everyone blocks the road: pedestrians dawdle about wherever they want, traffic or not; thus more hooting. Ornate remembrances of the raj or a crumbling Mughal temple, or now and then a silken-saried lady with a paunchy escort, stand out against the dereliction and exhaustion of it all.

Sally Belfrage, *Flowers of Emptiness*

Talking points

- The author begins her description by saying that she is describing 'the worst sight in the world'. What makes Bombay so horrifying to her?
- Amongst all the poverty, Sally Belfrage notices some signs of wealth. What are they? Do they make the scene any less horrible?

On his journey through America, Bill Bryson visited Las Vegas. In this extract, he describes his first impressions of the gambling capital of the world.

Las Vegas

I got to Las Vegas and my unease vanished. I was dazzled. It's impossible not to be. It was late afternoon, the sun was low, the temperature was in the high eighties, and the Strip was already thronged with happy vacationers in nice clean clothes, their pockets visibly bulging with money, strolling along in front of casinos the size of airport terminals. It all looked fun and oddly wholesome. I had expected it to be nothing but hookers and high rollers in stretched Cadillacs, the sort of people who wear white leather shoes and drape their jackets over their shoulders, but these were just ordinary folks like you and me, people who wear a lot of nylon and Velcro.

The names on the hotels and casinos were eerily familiar: Caesar's Palace, the Dunes, the Sands, the Desert Inn. What most surprised me – what most surprises most people – is how many vacant lots there were. Here and there

Travellers' tales

among the throbbing monoliths there were quarter-mile squares of silent desert, little pockets of dark calm, just waiting to be developed. When you have been to one or two casinos and seen how the money just pours into them, like gravel off a dump truck, it is hard to believe that there could be enough spare cash in the world to feed still more of them, yet more are being built all the time. The greed of mankind is practically insatiable, mine included.

I went into Caesar's Palace. It is set well back from the street, but I was conveyed in on a moving sidewalk, which rather impressed me. Inside the air was thick with unreality. The décor was supposed to be like a Roman temple or something. Statues of Roman gladiators and statesmen were scattered around the place and all the cigarette girls and ladies who gave change were dressed in skimpy togas, even if they were old and overweight, which most of them were, so their thighs wobbled as they walked. It was like watching moving Jell-O. I wandered through halls full of people intent on losing money – endlessly, single-mindedly feeding coins into slot machines or watching the clattering dance of a steel ball on a roulette wheel or playing games of blackjack that had no start or finish but were just continuous, like time. It all had a monotonous, yet anxious rhythm. There was no sense of pleasure or fun. I never saw anyone talking to anyone else, except to order a drink or cash some money. The noise was intense – the crank of one-armed bandits, the spinning of thousands of wheels, the din of clattering coins when a machine paid out.

A change lady Jell-O'd past and I got $10 worth of quarters from her. I put one in a one-armed bandit – I had never done this before; I'm from Iowa – pulled the handle and watched the wheels spin and thunk into place one by one. There was a tiny pause and then the machine spat six quarters into the pay-out bucket. I was hooked. I fed in more quarters. Sometimes I would lose and I would put in more quarters. Sometimes the machine would spit me back some quarters and I would put those in as well. After about five minutes I had no quarters left. I flagged down another ample-hipped vestal virgin and got $10 more. This time I won $12 worth of quarters straight off. It made a lot of noise. I looked around proudly, but no one paid any attention to me. Then I won $5 more. Hey, this is all right, I thought. I put all my quarters in a little plastic bucket that said Caesar's Palace on it. There seemed to be an awful lot of them, gleaming up at me, but in about twenty minutes the bucket was empty. I went and got another $10 worth of quarters, and started feeding them in. I won some and lost some. I was beginning to realise that there was a certain pattern to it: for every four quarters I put in, I would on average get three back, sometimes in a bunch, sometimes in dribbles. My right arm began to ache a little. It was boring really, pulling the handle over and over, watching the wheels spin and thunk, thunk, thunk, spin and thunk, thunk, thunk. With my last quarter I won $3 worth of quarters, and was mildly disappointed because I had been hoping to go for dinner and now here I had a mittful of quarters again. So

69

Part One–Genre

I dutifully fed the quarters into the machine and won some more money. This really was getting tiresome. Finally, after about thirty minutes I got rid of the last quarter and was able to go and look for a restaurant.

On the way out my attention was caught by a machine making a lot of noise. A woman had just won $600. For ninety seconds the machine just poured out money, a waterfall of silver. When it stopped, the woman regarded the pile without pleasure and began feeding it back into the machine. I felt sorry for her. It was going to take her all night to get rid of that kind of money.

I wandered through room after room trying to find my way out, but the place was clearly designed to leave you disoriented. There were no windows, no exit signs, just endless rooms, all with subdued lighting and with carpet that looked as if some executive had barked into a telephone, 'Gimme 20,000 yards of the ugliest carpet you got.' It was like woven vomit. I wandered for ages without knowing whether I was getting closer to or further from an exit. I passed a little shopping centre, restaurants, a buffet, cabarets, dark and silent bars where people brooded, bars with live music and astonishingly untalented entertainers ('And gimme some astonishingly untalented entertainers while you're at it'), and one large room in which the walls were covered with giant TV screens showing

Travellers' tales

live sporting events – major league baseball, NBA basketball, boxing matches, a horse race. A whole wallful of athletes were silently playing their hearts out for the benefit of the room's lone spectator, and he was asleep.

I don't know how many gaming rooms there were, but there were many. It was often hard to tell whether I was seeing a new room or an old room from another angle. In each one it was the same – long ranks of people dully, mechanically losing money. It was as if they had been hypnotised. None of them seemed to see that everything was stacked against them. It is all such an incredible con. Some of the casinos make profits of $100 million a year – that's the kind of money many large corporations make – and without having to do anything but open their doors. It takes almost no skills, no intelligence, no class to run a casino. I read in *Newsweek* that the guy who owns the Horseshoe casino downtown has never learned how to read and write. Can you believe that? That gives you some idea of the sort of level of intellectual attainment you need to be a success in Vegas. Suddenly, I hated the place. I was annoyed with myself for having been taken in by it all, the noise and sparkle, for having so quickly and mindlessly lost thirty dollars. For that kind of money I could have bought a baseball cap with a plastic turd on the brim *and* an ashtray in the shape of a toilet saying 'Place Your Butt Here. Souvenir of Las Vegas, Nevada.' This made me deeply gloomy.

I went and ate in the Caesar's Palace buffet, hoping that some food would improve my outlook. The buffet cost $8, but you could eat all you wanted, so I took a huge amount of everything, determined to recoup some of my loss. The resultant plate was such a mixture of foods, gravies, barbecue sauces and salad creams that it was really just a heap of tasteless goo. But I shovelled it all down and then had an outsized platter of chocolate goo for dessert. And then I felt very ill. I felt as if I had eaten a roll of insulation. Clutching my distended abdomen, I found my way to an exit. There was no moving sidewalk to return me to the street – there's no place in Las Vegas for losers or quitters – so I had to make a long weaving walk down the floodlit driveway to the Strip. The fresh air helped a little, but only a little. I limped through the crowds along the Strip, looking like a man doing a poor imitation of Quasimodo, and went into a couple of other casinos, hoping they would re-excite my greed and make me forget my swollen belly. But there were practically identical to Caesar's Palace – the same noise, the same stupid people losing all their money, the same hideous carpets. It all just gave me a headache. After a while, I gave up altogether. I plodded back to my motel and fell heavily on the bed and watched TV with that kind of glazed immobility that overcomes you when your stomach is grossly overloaded and there's no remote control device and you can't quite reach the channel switch with your big toe.

Bill Bryson, *The Lost Continent*

Part One – Genre

Talking points

- This description of Las Vegas provides a stark contrast with the earlier description of Bombay. In your group, make two lists – one for Bombay and the other for Las Vegas – and write down all the differences between them.

- The author of this extract finds the gaming machines in Las Vegas boring, and yet thousands of people visit them every year. Why do you think they do?

- Would you enjoy a visit to Las Vegas? What do you think you would like or dislike about it?

Suggestion for writing

This description would not please the Las Vegas Tourist Board!

Write a description of Las Vegas, based on this account, that *would* please the Tourist Board. You could write this in the form of a leaflet to be given to tourists considering a visit to the city, or an advertisement for Caesar's Palace casino.

In the winter of 1985, Robert Chesshyre returned to Britain after four years in America. A great deal had changed, and he found that he was seeing his native country with fresh eyes.

He set out to rediscover Britain and decided to visit Skelmersdale, one of the most deprived areas of the country. Skelmersdale is a new town outside Liverpool: people had been encouraged to move there from the Liverpool slums in the 1970s. It is known to the locals as 'Skem'.

Skelmersdale

Mine was the only car in the parking area for those shops, behind which litter and refuse piled up, giving the appearance of a shoreline on which a rubbish barge had been wrecked. Much of Skem is like that. Tons of waste must be dropped daily: the casual coke and beer cans, the fish 'n' chip papers, the plastic bags, the more purposefully dumped black dustbin bags, their contents spilling kitchen waste through gashes made by dogs. The animals are kept in their thousands to guard homes against the house-breakers who haunt Skem. Each morning the dogs are turned loose to foul every path and walkway: my introduction to the town had been a huge dog turd slowly dissolving in the rain on the bottom step of a chipped and scabietic stairway up which shoppers passed. A small boy asked if he could 'mind' my car: feeling intimidated, and visualizing a mighty scratch if I said 'No', I agreed, and he was suddenly idiotically pleased. 'Oh, I love minding cars, mister,' he said grinning. I decided to give him 50p rather than the 30p I first had in mind, and was genuinely disappointed not to find him at his post when I returned. (The worst that happened to my car was that someone pinched an American football 'Superbowl' bumper sticker, fresh from New York. 'You were lucky,' said a Lancashire citizen later, 'that they didn't take your wheels.')

Amenities are wretched beyond compare. There is no hotel, nor so much as an ordinary café. The health authorities had closed a Chinese restaurant, and the premises had become an 'amusement' arcade. There were a few run-down fish 'n' chip shops. I met a Londoner who had come from a poor area south of the Thames, where he had been accustomed to having takeaway food shops on his doorstep. He was amazed in his new home to find that he couldn't slip out for a hamburger at nine o'clock at night. Skem's two outlying shopping centres were dismal: the busiest shops by far were the sub-post offices, where

Part One—Genre

supplementary benefit Giros were exchanged; queues formed long before they opened. In one there was a rack of worn, cheap second-hand clothes in a corner. Jumble sales were advertised in nearly every window. Graffiti were everywhere, painted, scratched, etched into concrete, drawn, spray-gunned. Most of them were simple names, assertions that in this abandoned town in the middle of nowhere there were human beings who could define their existence on walls, doors, stairways. Sometimes there were plus signs between the names – 'Donna + Frankie + Cheryl' – as if together they could mean something, could make a difference. The competing graffiti were mainly concerned with football – Everton and Liverpool being as much a passion in Skem as they are in Walton or Anfield.

The centre of the town is the Concourse, a white hangar-like construction which houses the town's principal shops. It is connected by an overhead metal walkway to Whelmar House, the hub of 'Dole-town' in that it contains all the essentials – the Housing Department, the Job Centre, the DHSS benefits office. Teenagers with white, pinched faces, inadequately clothed against a biting wind, pushed babies across that clanking walkway, while below, the black taxis hooted and jostled. I sat in the Concourse, watching bored youths trying to set off bangers. Middle-aged women clutched plastic bags – 'You'll be impressed at Presto' and 'Buy British at Norweb' – and gossiped, ignoring both the youths and a tiny old man, with sunken cheeks, a cloth cap, a white tieless shirt buttoned at the collar, a filthy, cheap overcoat, worn black boots. He clutched a stick and stared into the middle distance, a survivor in a world not of his understanding.

Robert Chesshyre, *The Return of a Native Reporter*

Talking points

- In your group, discuss what impressions you got of Skelmersdale from this description. Make a list of ten words that seem to you to sum the place up.

- How do you think someone who lived in Skelmersdale might feel about this description?

- Do you think that Robert Chesshyre blames the inhabitants or the town planners for the condition of Skelmersdale? Here are some statements that you could consider in your answer:
    – Robert Chesshyre is already prejudiced against the inhabitants of Skelmersdale before he meets them.

- Any town with so much graffiti and litter must be full of ignorant and nasty people.
- The people of Skelmersdale take no pride in their surroundings.
- The people of Skelmersdale are poor; they cannot afford to look after their surroundings.
- The people could improve things if they wanted to.
- Robert Chesshyre describes the people as if they are utterly powerless.
- The only answer would be to knock Skelmersdale down.
- Skelmersdale was badly planned.

- Do you think that people behave differently according to their surroundings?

Suggestions for writing

1 Imagine that you could travel round the world in a split second and that you took five photographs as you went. What would the world look like in five snapshots? Describe in detail what might be in each photo. Use these descriptions to make a poem: each 'Picture' should be a stanza (or verse) on its own.

To help you get started, you could write a 'snapshot' of Bombay, Las Vegas or Skelmersdale. Here are a few lines from a 'snapshot' written by a Year 7 pupil:

A child is begging,
His clothes are ragged and dirty
With no shoes on his hard feet.

Make sure that your poem includes *contrasting* descriptions. You may find it helpful to watch a television news broadcast before you write.

2 It is quite likely that there are contrasting scenes (a noisy main road and a quiet park, or a tower block and a row of detached houses, for instance) in your own neighbourhood. Write two descriptions that bring out the contrasts between them.

Part 2

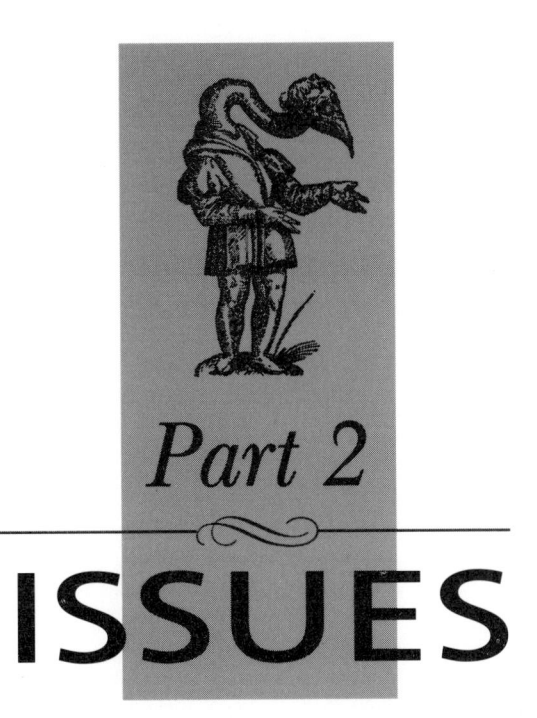

ISSUES

ANIMALS

Many young people are concerned about animal welfare, and an increasing number are deciding to become vegetarians. There is no doubt that many people, particularly young people, feel that eating meat is wrong.

In this unit, you will be reading a variety of extracts from autobiographies, newspaper articles and pamphlets, which argue the case for and against the eating of meat. Because most people in this country do eat meat, there are very few articles written in favour of meat eating. However, the Meat and Livestock Council represents the interests of meat-rearing farmers and therefore expresses the view that meat should be an important part of our diet.

Part Two—Issues

Start this unit by finding out how many of your class are vegetarians or have ever thought about being one. If you eat meat, are there any kinds of meat that you would not eat?

In a small group, read down this list. When the first person says 'Yeuch!', try to work out why we find some animals delicious but cannot bear to eat others.

lamb
chicken
beef
pork
veal
rabbit
deer
dog
snail
frog
cat

Betty the Hen

In this extract from her autobiography, Evelyn Cowan writes about a painful childhood experience that may well have made her a vegetarian.

One day in that summer of 1929 my mother made an important discovery. We were not the only Jewish family on the Island of Bute. In the course of one of her shopping expeditions into Rothesay, she made the acquaintance of Mrs Nubilsky, whose husband ran a bicycle and pram-renting shop just opposite the putting green.

An equally important part of the conversation proved to be the fact that Mr Nubilsky was an accredited shochet, a man qualified to kill animals according to the laws of the Jewish religion. Ma was delighted to hear this. Because of the distance from our kosher butchers in Glasgow, the purchase of fresh meat created a major problem. Non-kosher food never entered our home. She permitted herself to buy newly-caught fish from the boats that tied up in the harbour. Milk and eggs were delivered from a farm nearby.

One of my married sisters occasionally loaded a parcel of egg loaves from the bakers in the Gorbals on to the old *Kyle-more*. With this we made do. But Ma had an irresistible urge to make real Shabbos dinner with chicken soup and all the trimmings. Off we went to see Mr Cross the poultry-farmer. I trotted along beside Ma. My small schoolgirl figure and her tall bulky shape threw contrasting shadows on the sunlit hedges.

It was a shimmering hot June day. And in all the years that have passed since then, memory makes it more brilliant each time I remember it.

Rolling heavily in her almost bandy walk, Ma trudged up the hot dusty farm road. 'This heat is firing my bunions,' she winced. Towards the end she limped badly. She adjusted her worn black leather shopper on her arm and shouted to a big rugged red-haired man, 'Goot morning. Are you Mr Cross?' He touched his cap. 'Morning, missus. Yes, I am.'

'I'm the woman from Libya on the Ardberg Road. I get all my eggs here.' Hens were clucking all round us. 'Oh, yes.' His freckled hand wiped the perspiration from his brow. 'I mind now. You're the lady with all those nice-looking daughters.'

Ma threw him a suspicious look. 'Never mind that. Have you got a good fat hen for sale?'

'Sure we have. But I don't usually sell 'em this way.' Mr Cross laughed. 'Going to start a farm in opposition to me?'

'No, tanks. I got plenty to do. I just want someting for the week-end dinner.' I scarcely listened to all this, enveloped as I was in my mother's long skirt. At first I peeped out in fear and then courageously put my hand out to touch the strutting parade. Ma ran her eyes over the noisy farmyard. 'Hey! There's a nice fat one.' She pointed to a lovely white regal-looking bird. 'How about that one?'

Mr Cross ran over and grabbed it. 'It looks all right to me. I don't see why you shouldnie have it.' Ma poked around in her purse. 'Well, just tell me how much it is, and I'll take it.'

'OK,' said the farmer. 'I'll go up the road to the house and gauge its weight, and then I'll wring its neck for you.'

'Don't do that, please,' Ma pleaded hurriedly. 'Say how much. And I'll take it in my shopping bag.'

'You mean you want it alive, missis?'

'Yes, please, Mr Cross. Just tie some string round its legs. And I'll pop it in the bag.'

As we rolled along the road home, I tried to help with the heavy bag. I put my hand up to lift an end. The hen's innocent blue eyes gazed down into mine. It was love at first sight. I called her Betty.

As I have said, I was the youngest of a poor widow's family. And it may sound incredible, but it is quite true when I say that I never possessed a doll, or for that matter, a toy of any description. There was no lack of love in our home. I felt safe and secure always. I loved my mother deeply. But she was just there, like the sun and the moon and the clouds in the sky, taken for granted.

Everyone fondled and cuddled me, the baby. I was bathed, romped and loved

Part Two—Issues

by all the older sisters and brothers. I longed for something of my very own. Betty the Hen was my first true love. She fulfilled my need. Within a few hours my two brothers, Wally and Jacky, made a little wooden hut surrounded by a wire pen for my pet. I painted the name 'Betty' in dark blue on white wood.

After meals, I brought out scraps of food for her. I even tried to clean and brush Betty's feathers. The bird seemed to thrive on all this attention. Her feathers looked whiter, her stature more regal than before. She clucked happily (I thought) whenever she saw me approaching. We gazed into each other's eyes. I said little. Young love does not need much conversation.

Betty had been bought from the farm on a Monday. On Thursday, Ma sent a message to Mr Nubilsky's house above the bicycle shop, to say his services were required that evening.

My two brothers and myself were out picking brambles for jam in the Skeoch woods all day Thursday. It had been a happy, carefree day. We were exhausted from the heat. I knew that Betty was well stocked with food and water. So I did not go round the back yard. We flopped into our threesome bed, and I lapsed into a heavy childish sleep.

The next morning, Friday, before breakfast, I discovered the little hut was empty. Not a sound from the yard. All was silence. I ran into the kitchen. 'Ma, for goodness, Ma. The hen's gone.'

Feathers flew in all directions. My mother was busy plucking. 'Ach, here it is. Surely you knew I wanted it for Shabbos dinner. As soon as it is cleaned, I will kosher it and start it in the big pot. For tomorrow is Sabbath . . . Saturday.'

I could not raise my eyes further to the bleeding mass on her lap. Surely that was not Betty! Feeling sick, I raced across the promenade to the shore. I threw pebbles aimlessly in the water. Small waves rippled back at me. I thought of my make-believe puppy and the old stray cat I'd wanted for my own. Yet I never dreamed of begging for Betty's life. We were a large, hungry family. Although I had deluded myself for a short time, I knew in my young-old heart that Betty was for eating. I kicked my thinly-clad foot against a rock until my toes almost bled.

On Saturday morning I awakened on a pillow of grief. It was Shabbos, a quiet day, when no rough games were allowed. You had to keep your clothes in Sunday-best condition. Time dragged by. At last I heard my mother's voice echoing across the promenade. 'Children, keender, come on, now! Wash your hands and get ready for Shabbos dinner.'

We filed into the seldom-used dining room. Each child went to his or her place. After Kiddush wine and a little prayer murmured by all, we were served steaming plates of chicken soup with little knaidle doughballs dancing about on the surface. I turned away from this, the fragrant essence of my love. Then came the main course. This was stuffed roast chicken carried in on a large platter surrounded by 'cholent' brown potatoes and green vegetables.

Eagerly plates were pushed at Ma from both sides of the long table.
'I like the leg,' shrilled Wally.
'Give me the wing,' cried Jacky.
Cannibals! I raged into myself. My own brother, too! Uninvited, a piece of white meat appeared in front of me. I blinked down at it. My tears made a gravy on the plate.

Evelyn Cowan, Spring Remembered

Talking points

No doubt the author had eaten chicken many times before. Why couldn't she bring herself to eat this one?

Here are some statements about the extract. Which do you agree with?
- The author was sentimental.
- If you knew every animal that was killed for you, you wouldn't eat meat.
- The author couldn't eat the hen because she had given it a name.
- She would never eat meat again.
- She knows all along that the hen is for eating.
- Her mother is too cruel. She should not have killed and cooked Betty.
- The author should have persuaded her mother not to kill the hen.

When you have reached a decision, compare your views with those of other groups. Do you all agree?

Suggestions for writing

1. Write about a particular experience that made someone (it could be you) become vegetarian.

2. Write a version of this story as told by one of Evelyn's brothers. He has seen how she has become more and more attached to Betty. What might he expect to happen at the Shabbos (Sabbath) dinner?

   You could start your account with 'I knew that it would end in tears...'

Part Two—Issues

Space Sheep and Astro Pig

The leaflet on these pages was designed by the Vegetarian Society to encourage young children to become vegetarians. The activities that follow should be tackled either as part of a small group or with a partner.

Space Sheep & Astro Pig

TALK ABOUT

FACTORY FARMING

Some people may tell you that all farm animals lead a happy life in nice open fields, but this is not true.
Most of the animals I have seen are kept in cruel and horrible places called FACTORY FARMS.

Nearly all the hens are kept in tiny cages where they cannot even turn around or stretch their wings.
When they stop laying enough eggs for the farmer, he kills them.
They are then made into food like chicken soup or chicken pies.

I feel very sad and upset to tell you how my friends are treated.
The mummy pig, called a sow, is kept on a cold hard floor, where she has to give birth to her piglets.

She can hardly move as she is enclosed by metal bars, which stop her from reaching her babies properly. Her piglets are taken away from her too early, at only two weeks old.
Young and frightened, they are squashed into small pens where they are fattened.
They are killed before they reach six months old, for bacon, pork and ham.

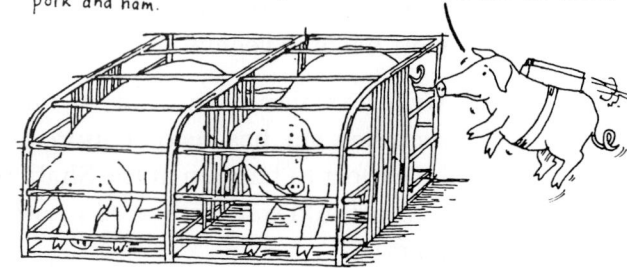

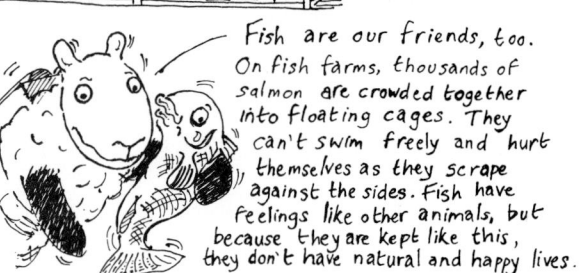

If you want to help stop this cruelty, only eat FREE-RANGE eggs. These eggs are laid by hens that are not kept locked up in cages.
Free-range hens lead a more natural and free life.

Fish are our friends, too.
On fish farms, thousands of salmon are crowded together into floating cages. They can't swim freely and hurt themselves as they scrape against the sides. Fish have feelings like other animals, but because they are kept like this, they don't have natural and happy lives.

84

Animals

These are only **three** types of animal that are mistreated in factory farms. We have seen ducks and rabbits locked in tiny cages, and baby calves and their mums (cows) and dads (bulls) crammed into pens where they never see a field in their life.

Many of these animals die in their cages, as they catch diseases and are very unhappy.

If you want to do something to help these animals, become a vegetarian.
Vegetarians are people who do not eat animals. Thousands of children are already vegetarians, why not join them?

If you want any more of these leaflets, and more info about going veggie, please write to:
The Youth Education team, The Vegetarian Society, Parkdale, Dunham Road, Altrincham, Cheshire WA14 4QG.

Or join our special club for junior members — you'll receive a goody bag full of leaflets, badges and stickers, as well as our brill *fab* magazine, Greenscene, 4 times a year.

By joining The Vegetarian Society, you'll be helping us to save animals, protect the environment and feed more people in poorer countries.
All this for only £4. So don't hang around — Send off the coupon on this page NOW!!

```
YES! I want to become a junior member of The Vegetarian Society
I enclose a cheque/PO for £4. (payable to The Vegetarian Society)
I am under 18.
Name: _____ Date of Birth: _____
Address: _____
_____
_____ Postcode: _____
```

Look out for the ᵛ symbol on food and other products. It means it is approved for vegetarians by The Vegetarian Society
100% Recycled paper   50M/2/93/KW

Part Two—Issues

Examining the evidence

Here are some things to consider in order to help you to see how the leaflet works:

Language
- Pick out any 'pleasant' words (e.g. nice) and any 'unpleasant' words. If any of the words have been altered by a negative (e.g. 'They can't swim freely'), put a line through the word like this: 'freely'

- What about the word 'factory'? You may not have picked it out. In your group, write down as many ideas as you can think of associated with the word 'factory'.
Now do the same thing with the words 'mummy', 'dad' and 'baby'.

- You have now studied all the words on the leaflet. What have you found out?

- In your group, write a statement about the way language is used in the leaflet. Explain why the writers have chosen to use certain words and the effect they are supposed to have on a young reader.
  Each group should read out its statement. Do you all agree?

Pictures
Here are some statements to help you to discuss the pictures. Which ones do you agree with?
- Space Sheep and Astro Pig are effective because children believe that animals can talk.
- The pig and the sheep are like cartoon characters.
- The hens in the cage look exactly the same as the free range hen.
- The animals are made to look human.
- The sheep and pig are meant to be space creatures.

- When you have discussed these statements, copy two or three animal pictures from the leaflet and draw thought bubbles coming out of the animals' heads. What might their thoughts be?

- Now try drawing pictures of a factory farm and farmer to accompany this leaflet. What would they have to look like? What would the farmer be thinking?

- Design a poster using Space Sheep or Astro Pig (or both) to persuade young children to become vegetarians. When you have completed it, write a short statement to explain how you designed the poster to appeal to young children.

Ideas
- Here are some statements taken from the leaflet. In your group, discuss whether you think they are true or not.
    - Some people tell you that all farm animals lead a happy life.
    - I feel very sad and upset to tell you how my friends are treated. (Astro Pig).
    - Fish are our friends too. (Space Sheep)
    - Fish have feelings like other animals.
    - Many of these animals . . . are very unhappy.
    - By joining the Vegetarian Society you'll be able to . . . feed more people in poorer countries.
- When you have discussed these statements, report your views to the rest of the class.

Suggestion for writing

Write a review of the leaflet, in which you comment on:
    the pictures
    the language and
    the ideas.
    Finish your review by saying how successful you think the leaflet is.
Would it persuade a child not to eat meat? Do you think the leaflet should be made widely available to children?

Part Two—Issues

The other side

Meat in the News is an educational news-sheet produced by the Meat and Livestock Commission to encourage young people to eat meat. You might think this is unnecessary, but the MLC obviously feels that it must do something about the number of young people who are becoming vegetarian.

The following extracts from this news-sheet are obviously aimed at teenagers, whereas the leaflet from the Vegetarian Society was written for primary schoolchildren.

Before you read it, think about why the MLC chooses to aim its educational material at older students.

DEVELOPMENTS IN ANIMAL WELFARE

JOHN PRATT – Veterinary Adviser, Meat and Livestock Commission – explains how new regulations and guidelines are being developed to ensure the welfare of animals reared for meat production.

Close on 44 million sheep, 12 million cattle, 8 million pigs, as well as 128 million hens, ducks, and geese are kept on British farms. The **husbandry** systems under which they are raised vary from intensive rearing to extensive conditions.

Intensive systems were introduced around thirty years ago not only to increase production, but also in an honest attempt to raise animals in better conditions. One such intention was to reduce bullying (which, for example, can occur among groups of **sows**), while another aim was to ensure that each animal received its fair share of food.

Guidelines for the farmer

Nowadays, various 'Codes of Recommendation' for the care of all farm livestock, and legislation governing animal welfare, provide guidelines for the farmer as to the treatment of the millions of animals reared for meat production. Government veterinary officers check standards of welfare on farms, in auction markets and at abattoirs.

The climate of public opinion is rapidly changing regarding farm animal welfare. There are now demands that animals should be kept in more natural conditions, and that **intensification** – at first hailed as providing shelter and ready access to food and water – should be phased out. This is indeed beginning to happen in this country, and we can confidently claim that Britain leads the way in animal welfare.

Intensification v extensification

Keeping animals in 'natural' conditions conjures up an idyllic picture, in contrast it would seem, to those confined inside in close contact and sharing the same air space. True, infectious diseases may require control in confined conditions – but parasites can be a constant hazard on pasture grazed, for example, by **extensively** kept lambs. Ventilation and lighting are essential in most animal houses, while shelter – either natural or artificial – should be provided for stock kept outside.

No one system is ideal – even animals in the wild have their problems in obtaining food, evading predators and finding shelter. So **intensification** and **extensification** are not necessarily directly opposed issues. The problems are too complex for such easy labelling – and the ideal lies somewhere between the two.

Many people do not realise this, which is a pity. Possibly the reason for this is largely due to the fact that most people nowadays have lost any close links with the real countryside and the farming communities in it. Ever since the last century, more and more people have been moving away from the countryside to live and work in towns and suburbs. As a result, the urban-dweller is on the outside looking in. There is a need for closer genuine contacts between the town-dwelling consumer of foodstuffs produced on the land, and those people who make a living on farms producing meat and other food products. This would hopefully make for better understanding on both sides.

Researching animal behaviour

It is also unfortunate that many expressing views on the animal welfare issue suffer from making **anthropomorphic** judgements. They insist on attributing human feelings and reactions to the animal world – and this is not necessarily valid or helpful. Such misconceptions are slowly being corrected through the publication of research into animal behaviour. This research is being funded not only by the animal welfare societies – such as the RSPCA and the Humane Slaughter Association – but also by the Government and, increasingly, by the Meat and Livestock Commission.

The Meat and Livestock Commission is endeavouring, through its work programmes and various assurance schemes on the farm, in the auction market and in the meat plant, to provide the consumer with more and more meat which has been raised by methods which pay particular attention to high standards of welfare throughout the life of the animal.

Anthropomorphic
The attribution of human characteristics and emotions to animals.

Extensively
Free-ranging, outdoors.

Extensive conditions
Spacious accommodation for animals, normally in the open.

Husbandry
Method of rearing

Intensification
Husbandry of stock in close proximity, normally in purpose-built accommodation.

Intensive rearing
Keeping of animals in close association, normally inside.

Sow
Mature female pig having had at least one litter.

Part Two—Issues

Examining the evidence

Layout
- Here are some questions to help you to think about the way the article is organised on the page:
    - What do you think of the layout of the page? Is it attractive? Clear?
    - Does the picture add to your understanding of the text?
    - Why is there a glossary?
    - Do you find the headline appealing?
    - Are the subheadings helpful?

Ideas
- Here are some arguments put forward by vegetarians.
    - Intensive farming is cruel.
    - Most meat is reared intensively.
    - Natural rearing of animals is less cruel.
    - The more the consumer knows about farming, the more shocked he or she is.
    - Animals feel pain and suffer in the same way as humans.
    - Farmers in general are not interested in improving the living standards of their animals.

    Does the article address these arguments? If so, how?

    Write the vegetarian arguments down in one column. Write the corresponding MLC arguments next to them like this:

Vegetarian view	**MLC view**
Intensive farming is cruel.	Intensive rearing reduces bullying.
	No system is ideal.

- Do you find the MLC article convincing?

Animals

Suggestions for writing

1 Adapt the MLC article into a leaflet aimed at a particular group of readers.

   Here are some ideas to help you:
   – You might think about working with a partner or in a small group rather than working alone on this project.
   – Think carefully about who you are writing for – your audience. You could choose one of the following:

   teenage girls
   teenagers of both sexes
   primary age children

   – Here is a table published by the MLC which you could use.

Variation in nutrient content of popular lunch-time snacks

Snack	Energy kJ (kcal)	Protein (g)	Fat (g)	Iron (mg)	Zinc (mg)
1 bag crisps, 1 can cola	1163 (278)	1.7	10.0	0.5	0.2
1 round Meat sandwich	1059 (253)	14.0	9.6	2.6	4.6
Chips, apple, tomato ketchup	2247 (537)	5.0	27.0	1.5	0.8

– Remember, you must make your leaflet look as attractive as possible so you will need to illustrate it with eye-catching photos. Women's magazines and Sunday supplements are good places to look for photos.

Part Two—Issues

2 Re-write the Vegetarian Society leaflet for a teenage audience. The leaflet as it stands is obviously aimed at young children. How could you get the same points across to an older and more sophisticated readership?
- Work with a partner, or as part of a small group.
- You may need to do some more research because an older readership will need more information.
- You will either need different characters or you will have to change the format altogether. Here are some formats you might consider:

    - Question and answer, e.g. 'How are most chickens kept?'
    - A guided tour of a factory farm.
    - Addressing the reader directly . . . 'Oy, you with the hamburger! Did you know that . . .?'

- Look for strong photos to add to the power of your argument. These are not easy to find and you may have to look for books on animal rights. Your library should be able to help you. If not, you may need to draw illustrations.

THE EFFECTS OF MR FORD

We are so used to a world that revolves around cars that we seldom stop to think about what it would be like without them. In this unit, you will be asked to look at the ways in which the car affects our lives. Should we be trying to use cars less? Are cars making children's lives unsafe and restricting their freedom?

Part Two—Issues

In 1982, Leroy Judson Daniels, an American horsetrader was 100 years old. His cousin, Helen Herrick, asked him to talk about his life, and she transcribed his taped autobiography. In the following extract, he describes a meeting he had with Henry Ford, the inventor of the mass-produced car.

Meeting Mr Ford

One spring I shipped a lot of good horses into Chicago. A potato grower came in with a friend to buy from me. I looked twice at that friend and I could see he was Henry Ford. Oh, that was a long time ago, must have been 1903 or 1904. I thought I was a pretty good horseman at that time. Ford's first car hadn't been out very long. You know, he had a buggy and put a motor in it, geared it up, that was his first car. Ford called his car a Quadricycle because it had four wheels. Awful-sounding name for anything a man's gotta depend on. He had a great dream about making a car for the middle-class people, one they could afford to buy. I asked Mr Ford, 'What do you think this car you've got will do? A horse can do anything a man needs, and everybody knows what to expect of him. This contraption you've got – I wouldn't know what it would do.'

Henry Ford said, 'This car is going to be a success. I'll make a car cheap enough so everybody can have one.' He did. I didn't get a car, not for years afterward, but he told me all about his Ford that day. He had taken the running gear of a buggy and put his own motor in it. No time to fool around building a body, the motor was what had to be invented. That was all they knew about making a car then, and Henry Ford was the only one who knew that. Anyway, I thought so. Others were trying, too, but he got there first, or at least cheapest. He tried it out, and he knew what he had when he talked to me. But I wasn't so sure.

'It's a success. You won't need horses anymore,' he said.

To myself I said, 'I'll keep right on with my horses.'

We had a long talk that day. In the period 1903 to 1904 alone, I found out later, Ford sold 1,700 cars. That doesn't seem like very many cars today, but then it was more than you could imagine. Like selling 3,400 horses, and wagons to go with those two-horse teams. Amounted to way over a million dollars, but I don't know how much it cost to build them. You'd have to figure it all in to see how much profit he made. But with the horse, you only figure what he cost when you bought him and what you might've had to feed him when you fattened him and rested him, or gentled him if he'd been wild before.

It gave a man something to consider, but the more I considered, the less I believed. 'How about that gasoline engine?' I asked. 'All that smoke's enough to kill a man. Get into the barn with the door shut and it'd kill you sure.'

The effects of Mr Ford

'Oh, no,' he laughed. 'But you remind me of something. You know, I've worked out a number of different engines trying to get just the right one for my car. I got a neat little one-cylinder motor, funny little thing, more like a toy, wanted to try it out, middle of the night, so I took it into my wife's kitchen and clamped it onto the sink. I was all set to start it up, but my wife wouldn't let me. She had our baby boy asleep in the next room, and she thought the exhaust from that engine would kill him, and the fumes would poison him.'

Ford laughed, but I wasn't so sure. 'What if all those fumes, after a few years, stay in the air, fill the air with that gasoline smoke?'

'Oh, can't hurt anybody,' he said. 'Just blows away in the wind. Man's been burning campfires for thousands of years – railroad engines, steamboats, factories – all kinds of fires for a good many years, and nothing's happened. Why would this little engine make any difference?'

I didn't know why. 'How about the steam engine?' I asked. 'Wouldn't that be cleaner?'

Ford didn't think they were practical. 'If it stinks up the air, we'll cross that bridge when we come to it. I hope it won't be a problem.' He looked thoughtful as he said all these things, and I felt better. At least he wasn't just doing whatever would bring him money. He wasn't forgetting about all the

Part Two—Issues

things that might happen. He was quite a bit older than I was, and he should have known what he was doing, he'd had time to figure it out. He explained how gasoline was refined and produced from the petroleum that was so abundant throughout the world, what a lot of jobs that would make, aside from all the jobs making automobiles and even making the wheels with rubber tires instead of the old iron ones.

'Besides,' he said, 'speaking of dirt, how about all that manure from horses that dries up and blows into everybody's faces? How about the muddy streets that we have to wade through so many months of each year? How about the flies and other insects that crawl everywhere?'

I could admire Ford, but my best thing was the horse, and I stayed with him. I wasn't so sure, not at all, and a lot of other people felt the same as I did, though a lot of others were buying cars as fast as they were produced. Didn't affect my business at all, not for a long time, a very long time. But there came a day . . . but now I'm getting ahead of my story, way ahead.

I had a lot of good horses there, and the man Ford was with bought about half of them. Maybe Ford hadn't convinced his friend either. That all happened a long time ago. I was just a young fellow trying to start my life, and I was glad for that sale. But I often think of what Henry Ford said that day: 'Mr Daniels, the days of horses are over. They're coming to an end. Sometime, maybe not soon, but not too long, machines will take the place of the horse. Automobiles first will take the driving horses away. Other machines will appear after that and do the work the horse does today cleaner, safer, don't have to feed them when they don't work.' I guess I grinned a little too wide when he said that, but he was right, to a certain extent. He knew what he was talking about, he had vision and instinct – to a point. I couldn't prove he was wrong, I only thought so, and I thought about it a lot, for a long time after that day.

Henry Ford was a tall man and not very good looking. He was dressed neat, but his hands were black. He was sort of a blacksmith to start with. He made that engine, kept making it a little better and a little better. Finally got a car that everybody could afford and no trouble with them wearing out, they lasted. First cars he put out you could buy for three hundred fifty dollars! A few years later Ford cars came out with brass all over them, covered with it! You could hardly look at a Ford, it was so bright. I bought my first car before that bright one showed up. Bought it from Rowley Thomas. Quite a thing to own a car those days.

Leroy Judson Daniels, *Tales of an Old Horsetrader*

The effects of Mr Ford

Examining the evidence

- How convincing is Henry Ford in the extract?

Take a piece of paper and divide it into two columns: **Advantages** and **Disadvantages**. In your group, discuss the advantages and disadvantages of the car and fill in the columns.

Are there more advantages than disadvantages, or more disadvantages than advantages? Present your findings to the rest of the class.

Suggestion for writing

Imagine that Henry Ford has asked you to advertise the first cheap, mass-produced car. How would you set about it?

Devise a series of posters that will persuade people to sell their horses and buy a car.

Part Two—Issues

From home to school

The article from *The Guardian*, below, describes the modern day results of Henry Ford's vision. As you will see, pollution isn't the only problem caused by traffic.

Rebecca Smithers reports on a call for transport policy to take account of needs of the young

Safety fears prompt parents to limit children's mobility, research shows

Massive growth in car ownership and stricter parental supervision are hampering children's development and mobility, according to a report published today.

The Policy Studies Institute claims that children are being increasingly brought up in the equivalent of "battery-reared" conditions because of parents' safety fears coupled with a growing dependence on cars, and argues that transport policy should take more account of the needs of children.

It is a follow-up to an institute study, produced two years ago, which showed that over the last 20 years there has been a slump in the proportion of children allowed to cross roads, go to school and visit friends on their own. The institute claims its two research projects, carried out in 1971 and 1990 at the same British schools, make up the only comprehensive study into children's mobility.

Now parents spend more time chauffeuring their able-bodied children around, denying them the opportunity to use healthy forms of transport such as bicycles, the institute says. It claims the main reason for parents wanting to escort their children home from school is the danger of traffic.

"We are not pointing the finger at parents," stresses Dr Mayer Hillman, who edited the report. "But growing car ownership has led to more fears about road safety, and we are worried about the long-term effects if children are not allowed to get around independently of adults."

Dr Hillman says that insufficient freedom from adult supervision slows down the development of "coping skills, self-esteem, a sense of identity and the capacity to take responsibility".

More than 20 years ago in 1971, 80 per cent of seven and eight-year-olds travelled to school on their own, compared with only 9 per cent now. Nearly four times as many children were driven to school in 1990 as 1971.

Dependence on the car, and the preponderance of a second car in many households, has led to cheap and healthy forms of transport such as cycling being "grossly underused", the report claims. It is virtually the only form of mechanised transport that children can use themselves, yet while 80 per cent of schoolchildren own a bicycle, only 2 per cent cycle to school.

In Britain, boys aged 11–15 make 13 per cent of their journeys by bike and girls 4 per cent. In the Netherlands, figures for the 12–14 age group are 61 per cent and 60 per cent respectively.

The report points out that children's social and emotional development is being hampered by constant adult supervision, while the lifestyles of parents are also being restricted by the need to escort their offspring.

It urges the Government and local authorities to consider changes of transport policy, with more emphasis on walking and cycling, and "traffic calming" measures and more community-centred activity.

Some of the options advocated are more "play streets" where cars are banned, more cycle routes and paths, and special zones where child pedestrians are given priority over motorists.

The institute questions road safety campaigns aimed at children, which, it claims, seek to "inculcate fear and attitudes of deference to traffic".

Children, Transport and the Quality of Life, edited by Dr Mayer Hillman; published by The PSI; £10

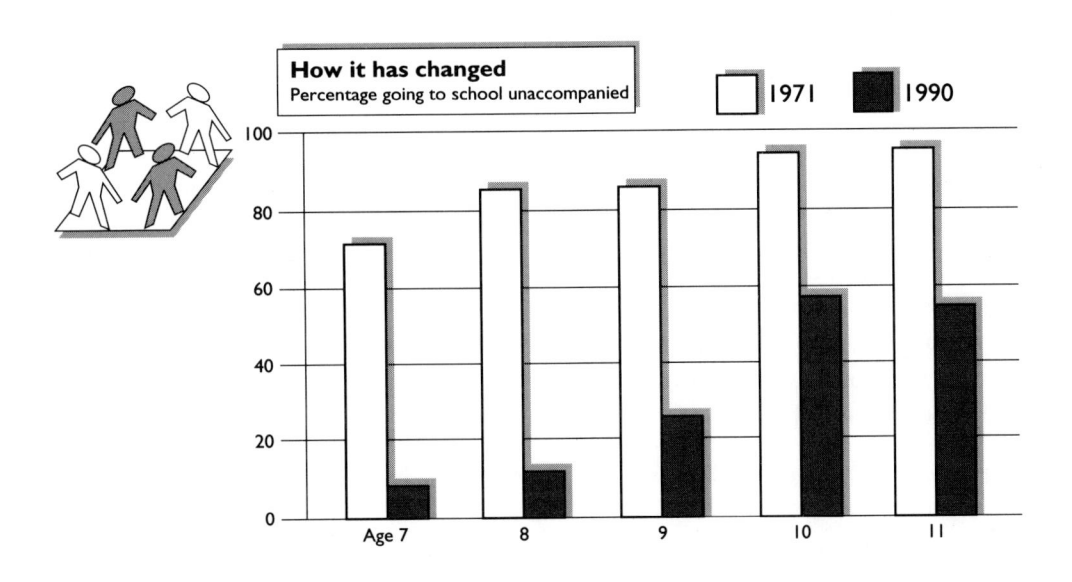

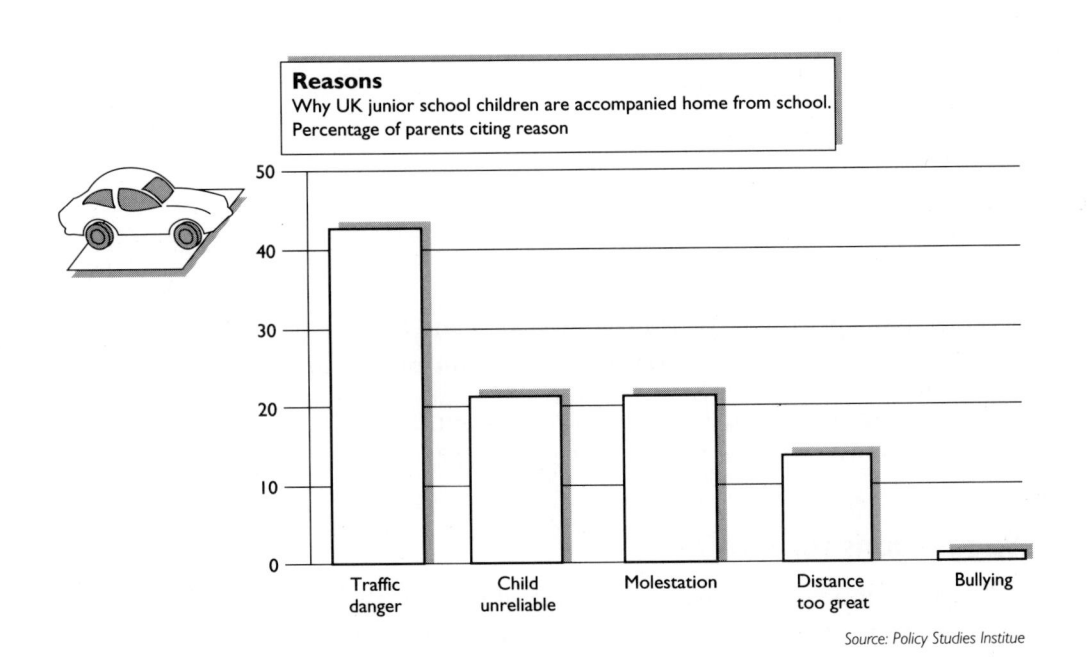

The effects of Mr Ford

How it has changed
Percentage going to school unaccompanied

☐ 1971 ■ 1990

Age	1971	1990
7	72	9
8	86	13
9	87	27
10	95	59
11	97	57

Reasons
Why UK junior school children are accompanied home from school.
Percentage of parents citing reason

Reason	%
Traffic danger	43
Child unreliable	22
Molestation	22
Distance too great	14
Bullying	2

Source: Policy Studies Institue

Part Two–Issues

Examining the evidence

- Here are some subtitles that could be used to break up the article. Where should they go?

    Parents not to blame

    Children not cycling enough

    Changes needed

    Children 'battery-reared'

- 'Safety fears prompt parents to limit children's mobility, research shows' is not the most eye-catching headline. If you were going to publish this article as part of a local newspaper report, what would be a good, powerful headline?

- The article suggests that some streets should become 'Play Streets', there should be more cycle routes and 'special zones' in which child pedestrians have priority. Using a map of your local area, decide where these should be.

    Each group should give a presentation to the rest of the class, putting forward its proposals for an environment which is more friendly to pedestrians.

- When were *you* first allowed out alone without an adult? In your group, discuss at what age you were allowed to:
    - go to school unaccompanied
    - visit friends
    - go shopping

    Do you think these were the right ages?

- How many people in your class or year come to school on their own? How many of them cycle regularly or go shopping unaccompanied?

Make up a questionnaire and ask other students to fill it in. How do your findings compare to the figures in the article?

Suggestions for writing

1 Start a campaign that will let more children be allowed out alone. The campaign is to be called: **Give the streets back to the kids!**

The effects of Mr Ford

a) Write a letter to your local council or local newspaper in which you argue that they should put some of the Institute's proposals into practice in your area. It might be a good idea to focus on one specific proposal (a play street, for example). You must make your letter as persuasive as possible. You should quote from the Institute's study and the Department of Transport report to add weight to your arguments.

b) Devise a publicity campaign that will include posters and leaflets to be given out to parents at the school gates. How would you persuade them to allow their children to cycle or walk unaccompanied to school?

ONE FALSE MOVE AND YOU'RE DEAD.

BEFORE YOU CROSS THE ROAD. STOP AT THE KERB.

101

Part Two—Issues

c) Write a short play or other entertainment (song, dance) to be performed in a whole-school assembly. Your performance should highlight the problems facing children and parents and suggest ways of overcoming them.

Be as imaginative as you like. Your play does not have to be realistic to get its points across. You could make it funny or outrageous – think about all those overweight, unhealthy kids being ferried around by irritated parents!

2 Imagine that cars have finally disappeared from our streets and are now only to be found in museums. A teacher is leading a school party around the museum, and they come upon a car. Write a short story or play in which the teacher tries to explain how the car worked and why it became obsolete. You could have the pupils asking awkward questions.

Computer Games

What adults think

Because computer games have only been in existence for a short time, many adults are suspicious of them.

SUPER NUTRENO™
ENTERTAINMENT SYSTEM
WITH
LUCKY LIZARD
EVERYDAY LOW PRICE £119.97
£99.97
WITH IN-STORE COUPON
SAVE £20

ONLY SOLD AT SUPER TOYS

POWER STRANGERS
SAGE master drive™
ONLY £99.99

Part Two—Issues

Working with a partner, note down all the concerns that you have heard expressed about computer games.

When you have made your list, compare it with the lists of other groups. Did you all come up with the same things?

Make a final whole-class list entitled 'What's Wrong with Computer Games'. Keep it to refer to later.

Now read the articles on pages 104–7.

The Sega sickener

Outrage at video nasty that makes a game out of 'real life' women being mutilated

A gruesome computer game depicting murder and torture was condemned by MPs yesterday.

Thousands of youngsters have already placed orders for Night Trap, which is expected to take Britain by storm when it is launched next month by the video games giant Sega.

Unlike the company's most famous video adventures – featuring the inoffensive Sonic the Hedgehog – the new game involves the horrific murder of five semi-naked actresses.

They are killed by being drilled through the neck and mutilated by sharp electric clamps.

Teenagers playing the game have to try to save them by fighting off psychopathic servants and monsters.

To add to the horror, Sega has used the latest 'virtual reality' technology to make the actresses appear real, rather than cartoon characters.

The technology allowing the inter-action of 'real' people and graphics comes with the company's new Mega CD, a high-tech compact disc player which plugs into a TV screen. The console, which has 500 times more power than a normal games unit, can also reproduce speech and music.

The results on screen are chilling images which appear more like a video nasty than a game.

More than 70,000 of the £270 consoles have been sold in Britain so far and retailers have been swamped with advanced orders for Night Trap. One said last night: 'This could well be the best-selling game of the year. Interest is vast. So are advance orders.'

Four of the actresses featured in the gruesome adventure are unknowns. The fifth is American star Dana Plato, who played Kimberley in the American TV comedy series Diff'rent Strokes.

In the game she is hung upside down in a cupboard while her blood drips into a –bottle. She also has to fight off ape-like monsters called Oggers.

During the compact disc adventure, which costs £50, the actresses wear skimpy shorts, low-cut nightdresses and revealing underwear.

Sir John Wheeler, Tory MP for Westminster North, described the game as 'abhorrent rubbish' and said he was disgusted with the manufacturers.

'The problem is that politicians who try to ban evil products like this only succeed in making them more popular,' he added. 'I am horrified.' Hayes and Harlington MP Terry Dicks, another Conservative, accused parents who let their children buy Night Trap of gross irresponsibility. 'I'm very concerned about this,' he said. 'The manufacturers are evil and ought to be punished for promoting the game.

'But I think parents are also responsible for letting their children buy this kind of filth.

'They should be forced to give their name and address if they buy it over the counter.'

Former Labour Party chairman John Evans, MP for St Helens North, called on the Home Office to investigate the game.

'The concept is absolutely horrifying,' he said. 'How can we allow such a dreadful thing to be freely available to youngsters? 'We have ratings for films so young people can be protected. We have a 9pm watershed on TV. We must urgently consider emergency controls on games like this which feature unacceptable levels of violence to women.'

Dame Jill Knight, Tory member for Edgbaston, Birmingham, said: 'This is a new generation of videos, nastier than ever before.

'I am extremely concerned to hear of this extraordinary new direction computer games are taking. We should consider legislation against such games because they encourage people to maim, mutilate and murder.'

Valerie Riches, from the pressure group Family and Youth Concern, said: 'This is a symptom of a very sick society. Our advice to parents is simply, "Do not buy this game for your children. It is evil."

'We also fear such graphic depictions of violence can, quite literally, blow young people's minds.'

A spokesman at Sega Europe's London HQ rejected the criticisms, however.

'They are plainly games in the context that they are in,' she said. 'We don't believe that games like Night Trap and Sewer Shark, which both use live actors, will have any adverse effect on players.'

The firm is also planning to use state-of-the-art graphics to bring out a new range of war games.

• A head teacher is being backed by parents after he barred hand-held video games from his school, saying they encourage playground violence. Clive Bourne, of Bredon Hill Middle School, near Tewkesbury, Gloucestershire, imposed the ban after finding that one in five of his 380 pupils brought the games to school and some were imitating the aggressive acts they depicted.

Luke Harding,
Daily Mail

Part Two—Issues

Dr Mario made me an addict

Playing the games is a lonely, obsessive activity, involving the total suspension of all normal life functions. While conscientiously researching this column, I idly picked up a Nintendo Game Boy to play Dr Mario, an abstract puzzle with a perfunctory medical theme that involves lining up capsules to destroy "viruses". Four hours later I emerged to find it was night, my neck had locked, my legs were without blood. Yet even writing that sentence made me want to go back and have another go. It was not enjoyable, it was merely necessary; I was not happy doing it, but for a brief period under the game's spell, I could not be happy not doing it.

Brian Appleyard, *The Independent*

HOOKED ON SONIC THE HEDGEHOG

Psychologists warn that video games are addictive and can make children withdrawn and introverted.

Although research is at an early stage, and based largely on American studies, there is evidence that combat games can also encourage children to be more aggressive.

Dr Mark Griffiths, a psychology lecturer at Portsmouth University who is conducting his own research, said children could become hooked on the machines in a matter of a few days.

'The world-wide research for young children, eight years and younger, suggests they show higher levels of increased aggression immediately after playing the games.

'But for teenagers that effect has not been proved.

'My intuition is that people who play every day for long periods of time do show higher levels of aggression.'

Dr Griffiths said addicted players will think about the games, and how to play them, even when they are not playing them. The "high" or "buzz" caused by the machine means the more they are played the more a child needs to play them.

But the games with an educational aspect do have a positive side and can stimulate children to think for themselves, added Dr Griffiths.

"The games are a fad but the people who are playing them now will be involved in technological advances in the future."

By Staff Reporter

Computer games

Gamegirl zapped

In the United States, the game market is evenly split between boy and girl consumers. No equivalent research has been done in the UK, but it is generally accepted that girl players are heavily outnumbered.

Critics such as Meenu Vora, responsible for a Tec (Training and Enterprise Council) initiative to encourage girls into computing, point out that branding computer games as a boy's thing perpetuates the problem. 'Half of all computer staff in the US are women, where the equivalent figure here is around 22 per cent and dropping,' said Ms Vora.

'It doesn't help if kids are made to feel, as young as six or seven, that computers are for boys. Nintendo claims its marketing is not gender-biased. Yet its hand-held machine is called Gameboy, and most of the games are to do with fighting, racing cars, flying planes... traditional boys' stuff.'

There is the odd girl's title, such as *Barbie Goes Shopping* in the Nintendo range, but it looks out of place next to *Streetfighter II*, *Brawl Brothers* and *Bad Dudes vs Dragon Ninjas*. 'Research shows boys are turned off if a product is marketed specifically at girls,' says a Nintendo spokeswoman, 'whereas girls will join in with boys' pursuits.'

Margie Thomas adds: 'If female characters appear in a game, it's usually at the beginning, where they get kidnapped. It's then your job to rescue them. I don't mind being Mario as he tries to save the Princess, but I don't see why it *always* has to be the guy saving the girl.'

Phil Dourado,
The Independent

Granny falls for the plumber

Kate Bevis's youngest children are at university, but during the holidays she has to unplug her hand-held machine between sessions to prevent them obliterating her last position once she sets it aside.

'I only allow myself three games at a time,' she says, sitting in her rambling Victorian semi in Barnet, north London. 'It's the most appalling waste of time and not even relaxing. It's fun for a very short time. But by the fourth time Mario has been eaten by some monster you lose your temper.

'But I'm totally addicted. With an addiction, though, you're supposed to get some simple pleasure. Not with this. It's very, very irritating. I even dream about it sometimes. And I certainly think about how I'm going to overcome the next hurdle when I get stuck. But while I can figure it out, I sometimes don't have the skill to make him do what's needed. That's the advantage the children have.'

Her children caused the problem by giving it to her, but her curiosity was first aroused when she noticed her fidgety choirboys had inexplicably become quiet. 'They had gleaming faces all of a sudden. Then I discovered that they were all playing their Nintendos with the sound turned down. I wanted a go, too.'

Now they're all at it. 'I even threatened to take mine along for the anthem,' she says, grinning. But then she becomes serious. 'Don't write anything that'll make me look like a loony or I'll never be allowed to take another funeral.'

Ian MacKinnon,
The Independent

107

Part Two—Issues

Look back at the list you made. Did you predict all the concerns expressed in the articles?

Examining the evidence

- In your group, take a large sheet of paper and give it the title, 'Critical Sheet'. On this, write down all the criticisms of games that are made in the articles. Write each critical statement on a different section of the paper.
  Underneath each statement, write a short summary of the reasons given for it in the article. For example:

> COMPUTER GAMES ENCOURAGE VIOLENCE
> A headmaster has found that children copy the violent acts they see on hand-held games etc....

You may not agree with these criticisms, but don't write down your own views for the time being. Only use the views expressed in the articles.

Keep this 'Critical Sheet' for further reference.

What is *the problem?*

Now read the following articles in defence of computer games.

Don't panic, it's only Dr Robotnik and the crystal egg zone

Jane Berthoud doubts if our children are being ruined by computer games

So what is the problem? Why do we love to hate computer games so much? Is it just the Nineties' version of the generation gap? Do we feel threatened by children of seven knowing more than we do at 37? Or is it really a case of mummy knows best?

Time spent with *Sonic the Hedgehog* can be obsessive, but no more than collecting football cards or doing jigsaws used to be. When I was about eight, I remember hours, days, weeks spent swapping 'scraps'. The whole process involved buying packets of glossy, garish, cut-out pictures of pussycats, girls pushing prams and large angels with enormous wings floating on clouds, and God knows what. These then had to be laid out carefully, one each, between the pages of books. If you already 'had' it, then the scrap was left sticking out of the top of the book so that you could spend endless playtimes sitting on the school wall swapping your swaps with friends.

True, there was some kind of sociable element, but probably no more than there is with kids who talk incessantly about their computer games. And I fail to see how buying pictures of angels with huge wings and no legs floating on clouds is creative, stimulating or educational.

Sonic, for the uninitiated, is a blue hedgehog with large eyes, pointed ears and bright red boots. He looks no more like a hedgehog than Super Mario looks like a plumber, but Sonic can run, spin through the air, fly a glider, loop the loop and break holes in brick walls at high speed.

There are seven levels to the game with three acts in each level, and I cannot even complete the first. *En route*, the hedgehog is supposed to collect six emeralds. I still haven't found one. I have no idea how to stop Sonic falling down the hole he has to jump across between the fifth and sixth brick walls in act one of level one, the underground zone. I am sure I shall never witness the treats of the sky-high zone, the aqua-lake zone, the green hills zone or any of the other tantalisingly named regions way beyond my capabilities. I shall never manage to help Sonic in his desperate bid to rescue his friend Tails – a two-tailed fox – from the evil clutches of Dr Robotnik. Somehow the Brothers Grimm will just have to do me for life.

Needless to say, both my children are way ahead of me. Their combined ages are roughly half mine, and yet they have worked out how to get Sonic to level five, the crystal egg zone, where at least three of the emeralds are. They also know how to spot which bits of wall Sonic can smash through in order to get into secret places. Now that is observation. That is skill.

The concentration required for all this is enormous. Each time you go wrong you have to go back to the beginning. I can survive 20 minutes maximum – they sit for hours. And even when you recognise what needs doing, it still requires maximum hand-eye co-ordination to press the right button at the right time.

How on earth can anyone condemn all this as meaningless, useless and time-wasting? Angels with enormous wings and no legs, yes. But Sonic, never. Children with epilepsy must clearly be warned of the dangers, but let's not over-react; computer games surely have their place in our children's education.

Part Two—Issues

Craze for Video Games

Sixth form student and computer fanatic, Dominic Porter defended computer games, insisting they weren't all about death and violence.

16-year-old Dominic, who had his first games machine when he was five said: 'I don't think computer games are a bad thing.

'I like them because they are a challenge, just like any sport.'

He said: 'A lot of the games are based in fantasy lands and it's like watching films, you imagine yourself in the character's place.'

Dominic admitted many games were violent but blamed society for that.

'That's what a lot of people want but hundreds of other games involve puzzles or tasks which make you think and use your imagination.' He added that he didn't think games made youngsters withdraw into themselves or become obsessive.

'There are lots of games which are for more than one person and are quite competitive. Also you talk to your friends about games and your score. Basically it's just a way of passing the time, just a hobby.'

Computer games

Examining the evidence

- Look at your 'Critical Sheet'. Are all the criticisms made there addressed in these two articles? Write down on your sheet what these writers have to say about games. Write the comments next to the appropriate statement.

- What do *you* think about computer games? During your discussion you may want to refer to your 'Critical Sheet' or the articles themselves. Don't forget to use your own experience as evidence.

  Here are some questions to help you in your discussion:
  - Are the games addictive?
  - Are games mostly aimed at boys?
  - Do you think that combat games make young children more aggressive?
  - Does playing games stop children doing other activities like reading or playing outside?
  - Do the games have any educational value?
  - Do you think some games should be 'Adults Only'?
  - Are some games insulting to women?

  When you have discussed these questions, report your views to the rest of the class.

Suggestions for writing

1 Write your own newspaper story on a computer games 'scare'. Make it as ridiculous and exaggerated as possible. Here are some suitably lurid headlines to get you started.

'Computer games ruined my life!' says Granny, 85

COMPUTER GAME ZOMBIES WRECK SUPERMARKET!!

'SONIC DUNCES' FAIL AT SCHOOL

New Game 'Horror Ghouls' to hit the market

Part Two—Issues

Include comments or reactions from some of the following: worried parents or relatives, a scientist who has recently completed some research, a local headteacher, an outraged MP.

2 Write a speech to be delivered to a Parent/Teachers Association (PTA) meeting in which you defend computer games. Make sure that you have arguments that will answer all the concerns that parents and teachers have about the games.

Computer games – language and names

Whatever your opinion of computer games, it is clear that they are here to stay. More and more shops are stocking them, and more and more households use them.

Computer games, like most other games, have their own language and their own set of names. The following two exercises look at the nature of this language.

Game language

The following words and phrases have special meanings for games players. By asking around the class, see if you can come up with definitions for all of them.

level
boss
sprite
playability
'Beat 'em up'
'Shoot 'em up'
platform
meg
joy pad
scrolling
graphics
zone
arcade game
role playing game (RPG)

Now write your own 'Game Players' Dictionary' in which you define these game terms in alphabetical order. Add other terms, and their definitions, to this dictionary, if you like.

Game names

The name of a computer game is one of the most important ways of attracting a potential buyer. Here are some genuine examples of the names of computer games:

> Black Hole Assault
> Ecco the Dolphin
> Sewer Shark
> Road Avenger
> Fantastic Dizzy
> Streets of Rage
> James Pond

You may know some of these games already. If not, could you tell what sort of game it was, just from the name?

Here is how the game 'Castlevania' is described in its advertisement:

> **CASTLEVANIA**
>
> – As John Morris, the whip-wielding vampire hunter, or Eric Lecarde, master lanceman, you'll chase the demonic vampiress, Countess Bartley, across Europe to prevent her resurrecting the master of all evil – Count Dracula.

Now try making up some game titles of your own. Next to each title write a description of the game like this one for 'Castlevania'. You can make your games as silly as you like (after all, the hero of 'Fantastic Dizzy' is an egg!).

What about inventing some games that are based on school life? Here are some possible titles:

> Teacher's Life
> Dinner Lady
> Headteacher's Holiday.

Write a description for each one. You could also devise a full-page advertisement for one of the games, to go in a magazine.

It NEVER DID *ME* ANY HARM

Should children be smacked or beaten when they do something wrong? Not so long ago, it was common for children to be caned or slippered at school. Nowadays it is illegal for teachers to beat children in state schools, although some independent schools still use corporal punishment. Many parents, however, smack their children and obviously feel that it does not permanently harm them.

In 1990, an organisation called EPOCH (End Physical Punishment of Children) decided to declare a No Smacking Week, beginning on New Year's Eve, as part of their campaign to make physical punishment of children illegal.

Part Two—Issues

Talking points

Should corporal punishment be used against children? Before you read any further, think about your own views and those of your parents and teachers. In groups, share and discuss these views. Here are some questions to help your discussion.

- Do you think that your teachers would use corporal punishment if they were allowed to?

- Do you think that many parents smack young children?

-
 Were you smacked when you were younger?

- How would you prevent young children from doing dangerous or destructive things?

- Do you think that smacking is cruel?

- Would you advise parents of ten or eleven year olds to use corporal punishment?

- Do you think that if teachers were allowed to beat children then pupils would behave better?

When you have discussed all these questions, report back to the rest of the class. Is there general agreement on certain questions? Which questions cause disagreement?

It never did me any harm

No smacking week

Here are two newspaper articles reporting the announcement of No Smacking Week. The first is from the Daily Mirror. Read it in groups of four, with each member of the group taking on one of the following roles.

- A parent who has recently smacked his or her toddler to teach him or her not to touch electric sockets.
- A teacher who feels that children these days are too disobedient.
- A man or woman who was beaten at school and remembers the pain and humiliation.
- A social worker who deals with cases of children who have been seriously injured by their parents.

Respond to the article in role. Each member of the group should take it in turn to speak.

Once you are sure how your character would react to the article, write a letter to the Daily Mirror, expressing your character's views. Remember, your letter must sound as if it was written by one of the four characters above. Make sure your views and language are appropriate.

Part Two—Issues

Pressure growing on parents who smack their kids

By Roger Todd

HEARD about the 11-year-old boy who reported his dad to the police for giving him a smack... and had him fined £10?

It happened in Sweden, but the day is approaching when it may be a crime to lay a hand on your kids here too.

A National No Smacking Week, beginning on New Year's Eve, will be announced tomorrow. It may sound like some kind of seasonal joke – but it is deadly serious.

The pressure group co-ordinating it, EPOCH (End Physical Punishment of Children), is campaigning to have smacking made illegal.

And Britain could soon be moving in the same direction as Scandinavia and Austria, where it is already banned.

The Department of Health is spending £200,000 on a study of child-beating and the right of parents to hit their kids is being probed by the Scottish Law Commission.

A commission spokeswoman said: 'It could result in an all-out ban on parents having the right to beat children.'

Dark

There is a lot of smacking going on. A nationwide study of the problem paints a dark picture. It shows that:

- Six parents out of 10 hit their one-year-old children.
- Nine out of 10 hit their four-year-olds.
- By the age of seven, one child in 12 was being hit by a parent at least once a day. A third were hit once a week, and 22 per cent were beaten with a belt, stick or other weapon.

The Department of Health-funded survey, starting in February, will try to find out the truth behind such disturbing statistics.

Children will be asked for the first time how they feel about being smacked, beaten, shaken, screamed at, caned, slippered, belted or battered.

Their parents will be asked why they did it, what they thought they achieved and how they felt afterwards.

Psychologists from London University's Institute of Child Health will try to discover whether hitting children makes them turn to violence to solve problems when they grow up.

Marjorie Smith, the psychologist running the study of 400 families in and around London, says: 'We're looking at the whole issue of parental control and its effect.'

'We will look at what happens to children aged one, four, seven and 11 and interview the two older age groups.

'We expect to interview all the mothers and about a quarter of fathers.

'We want to know whether children who have been subjected to physical punishment at home are more likely to use it themselves.

Violence

'And we want to know whether it makes a difference to children if they felt it was a "fair cop".'

The NSPCC is against smacking, and director

It never did me any harm

Chris Brown will support No Smacking Week at tomorrow's launch.

A spokesman says: 'A lot of parents who batter their children started off just smacking them.'

EPOCH's co-ordinator, Peter Newell, agrees: 'More than a quarter of parents lose control when they smack their children.

'They find the odd smack doesn't work, so the tendency is to escalate the severity of the beating.

'Thirteen per cent of local authorities said this was often the explanation for serious child abuse.

'The parents explained they were just using their right to hit their child. It started as ordinary punishment which got out of hand. One little girl from Bristol was beaten to death by her father because she couldn't spell her name.

'The message children get from being beaten by someone they love and respect is that it's a useful way of sorting out a problem.

'That leads them to become more likely to bully at school, to abuse their own partner later in life and get involved in violent crime.'

So how should you discipline children? Mr Newell, who has three young boys, says: 'Children love being praised. They won't always behave, but it's quite simple to explain why they have upset you or what they have done wrong.

'Unfortunately, what you tend to see – in supermarkets, for instance – is the child who behaves unspeakably being given sweets to bribe it into behaving.

'The child that does behave seems to be ignored. That is not giving it the right signals.

'If you praise and reward your children for doing good things you'll have them eating out of your hand.'

EPOCH has free leaflets on how to discipline your child without smacking. Write to: EPOCH, 77 Holloway Road, London N7 8JZ. Include a large SAE.

*Daily Mirror
December, 1990*

Models have been used for this photograph
Photo: NSPCC

Hands off! Suffering a few smacks from mum or dad can quickly turn into a violent nightmare for children even younger than these models

Part Two–Issues

Now read the following article from the Daily Telegraph which was published on the same day.

Parents urged not to smack children

By Michael Kerr, *Home Affairs Correspondent*

A NATIONAL No Smacking Week was launched yesterday by campaigners who hope it will persuade parents to give up corporal punishment for good. From New Year's Eve to Jan 6, EPOCH, the campaign to end physical punishment of children, wants parents to resolve not to smack their children.

The idea is supported by the NSPCC, which believes punishment can 'easily escalate into abuse', and other organisations such as the National Children's Home, the National Child-minding Association and the Voluntary Council for Under-Fives.

However, a teachers' leader said it was 'nonsense', and the pressure group Family and Youth Concern saw it as 'just another attack on parental rights and responsibilities'.

EPOCH is distributing leaflets asking parents to talk to each other, family and friends and find 'new ways of encouraging children to behave'.

A newspaper poll earlier this year found that nine out of 10 parents thought mild corporal punishment acceptable.

The Government has said there is no consensus that it is immoral or harms the child, though the Law Commission in Scotland is seeking views on whether smacking should be banned there, as it is in five European countries.

The childcare writer Penelope Leach, a founder of EPOCH, said most parents smacked their children as a matter of course. Unless they decided otherwise, their children would go on to hit their grandchildren:

'We want them to test out our claim just for a week, that children who are reared without violence and the fear of violence are easier to live with and discipline.'

Esther Rantzen, the television presenter, who helped to launch the campaign, said she smacked her children and regretted it. Though she was not close to her parents, she had lost respect for them and rebelled against them as a child over smacking.

But Mr Peter Dawson, general secretary of the Professional Association of Teachers, rued the disappearance of corporal punishment from State schools.

His daughters were grateful to him for being firm, he said. 'If you see your small child crawling towards the fire, a good smack will teach the child to keep out of the flames.'

The Daily Telegraph
December, 1990

It never did me any harm

Talking points

- The Daily Telegraph reported No Smacking Week in a different way from the Daily Mirror. In your group, see how many differences you can find. Can you tell whether or not the writer of each report is in favour of No Smacking Week?

- Imagine that you are the editor of the Daily Telegraph and have just received this article from one of your reporters. You decide that the writer is biased against No Smacking Week and that his report is too one-sided. The reporter feels that he has been perfectly fair. In pairs, perform a role-play, with one person taking the role of the editor and the other acting as the reporter.

  When you have completed your role-play, report to the rest of the class whether you found the article biased or balanced.

Part Two—Issues

Beatings at the Dragon

Most schoolchildren these days have no experience of being beaten by teachers. To enable you to understand what it might feel like to be punished in this way, read the following extract by Paul Watkins. At the age of seven, he was sent from his home in America to board at the Dragon School in Oxford. The teachers at the school are addressed as 'Pa' by the children.

After Pa Vicker had threatened to thrash me within an inch of my life if I ever lied, I swore that I would tell the truth for the rest of my life, no matter what had happened.

Then I got on the wrong side of Pa Pushcart, the gym teacher.

He was always yelling at me because I was slow changing for gym class.

On one of those slow days, I looked in my locker space and saw that my plimsolls had been stolen. I was late, so I grabbed the plimsolls from the locker belonging to Big Watty Dog Watkins* and put them on. We all had the same Green Flash Dunlops and I knew no one would notice.

As soon as we were all in the gym, Pa Pushcart lined us up against the wall. We knew there was some trouble, and out of instinct, our hands crept down to shield our balls.

Pa Pushcart's shoulder hunched the way a grizzly bear's shoulders hunch when it stands up on two feet. 'There are thieves among us,' he said.

God damn it, I thought. God damn it to hell, I am busted.

Then Pa Pushcart locked his hands behind his back and began to pace in front of us. 'There have been some instances,' he said, 'of people stealing other people's gym things. Shorts, T-shirts, shoes. And this thieving will stop, gentlemen. We will nip it in the bud and strangle it in the cradle. I want you to know right now that if anyone today is wearing clothing that belongs to someone else, I am going to beat them.'

I had the cramp of knowing-about-going-to-be-beaten in the small of my back and my bowels. Well God damn it, I thought again, at least I don't have to run and fetch my plimsolls the way Pa Winter made us do.

'You can make things a lot easier on yourselves,' Pa Pushcart told us, 'if you own up and admit you are wearing stolen clothing. Those of you who are, take one step forward.'

I stepped forward. The rest of the class seemed to have disappeared into the wall behind me. Suddenly I stood way out in front. I felt as if I was standing at the edge of a cliff.

---

*The nickname of another boy called Watkins.

It never did me any harm

'Watkins!' Pa Pushcart howled in my face. 'I might have known it was you. What did you take?'

'Plimsolls, sir.'

He took hold of the back of my neck and moved me over into the storeroom, where he kept the medicine balls and hemp mats and rope. He made me take off one of the stolen shoes and he started to give me the Six, keeping his hand on my neck.

But on the fourth, he stopped. 'Your name is *Paul* Watkins isn't it?' he asked.

'Yes, sir.' My butt was on fire. He was the hardest Whacker in the school.

'Well, you bloody idiot! I am beating you with your own shoe!'

Big Watty Dog Watkins had used his own plimsolls to make a Guy Fawkes dummy. Then he stole my shoes and put them in his locker. I stole them back but did not know they were mine.

I did some more thinking about my promise never to lie no matter what happened. I figured that from now on I would take it on a case-by-case basis.

Later on I learned that if you are going to get whacked whether you lie or tell the truth, well, Hell, you may as well enjoy yourself a little and the least you can do is be rude to the person who's whacking you.

I had made a tape recording during the holidays. On the tape were opening jingles to all the TV shows I watched while I was home.

The only thing I had to play them on was a clunky Panasonic.

I lay in my bed at night, covers pulled over my head, and listened to the jingles. I got to know them so well that they turned into one song. I sang them through without a pause.

One night as I listened, the sheets disappeared off my bed and Pa Vicker stood trembling angry in front of me. He had ripped back the sheets and now he let them drop to the floor.

He picked me up and led me by the arm all through the house, upstairs and down, stamping along the corridor and me hugging the Panasonic to my chest.

When we had gone past all the dorms, he turned to me and did what he usually did which was bring his face close to mine and breathe milk and tobacco breath in my face. 'Well now, Watkins. What did you hear?'

'What do you mean, sir?'

'What did you hear as we were walking around the house just then?'

'Nothing, sir.'

'And why do you suppose that was, Watkins?'

I knew what he wanted me to say. He wanted me to say that everyone was asleep. Then he would say I should be asleep too and he'd confiscate my Panasonic and maybe Whack me as well. I saw it all coming from miles away. But I didn't say what he wanted. Instead I told him – 'I guess it was quiet, sir, because you made so much noise walking up and down the halls. Not like you

123

Part Two—Issues

usually do, sir. You know, in your crêpe-soled desert boots. So they had time to shut up before you heard them. Sir.'

I was surprised he let me talk it all the way through.

He took the Panasonic. I just handed it to him. And he beat me, right there in the hallway. It was the first time he had beat me that I did not cry, and the last time a beating ever hurt.

I got beatings after that, for dumb things like talking in homework, but something in me took the pain away and kept my eyes dry and my teeth clamped shut so that the only sound I made was a quiet grunt as each blow came down.

It never did me any harm

Talking points

- Were you shocked by the severity of the punishment Paul Watkins received?

- Did being beaten teach the young Paul Watkins not to steal?

- Did it teach him not to lie?

- Why did the teachers beat him?

- Could the teachers have acted differently without losing respect?

- How did being beaten change Paul Watkins?

- If teachers at your school were allowed to punish pupils in this way, what do you think would change?

Suggestions for writing

1 Imagine that you have been asked to make a radio programme on the subject of corporal punishment to be broadcast at the beginning of No Smacking Week. The programme will include comments from the following people:

   – a spokesperson for EPOCH
   – Paul Watkins
   – a government minister
   – a teacher from a school that uses corporal punishment
   – a state school teacher (one of your own teachers?)
   – a spokesperson for the NSPCC
   – a pupil from a state school
   – a parent or grandparent (perhaps a real interview with your own)

Write a transcript of the programme. If you wish, use names from the extracts you have read in this unit. Set out your script like a play, with yourself as presenter.

When you have written your script you could tape it, using other members of your class to act as the various interviewees.

Part Two—Issues

2 Write a guide for new teachers at your school. Give it the title 'How to Get the Best from Pupils'. In the guide, explain how teachers should discipline pupils if they do something wrong. You might like to set it out in the form of questions and answers, e.g. 'What do I do if a pupil fails to hand in homework?'

Many schools publish handbooks for new teachers. When you have finished your guide, you could ask to see the real thing. How does yours compare with it?